A Model School

How Philadelphia's Gesu School is Remaking Inner-City Education

Also by Jerrold K. Footlick

Education–A New Era

The College Scene Now: Life, Learning, and Ferment on the American Campus Today

Truth and Consequences: How Colleges and Universities Meet Public Crises

The Awakening: Queens University of Charlotte–Yesterday, Today, and Tomorrow

Careers for the Seventies: Close-Ups of 20 Ways Americans Earn a Living (editor)

The Black Athlete: International Library of Negro Life and History (editor)

A Model School

HOW PHILADELPHIA'S GESU SCHOOL IS REMAKING INNER-CITY EDUCATION

BY
JERROLD K. FOOTLICK

VILLIGER PRESS
PHILADELPHIA

Cover photo © Suzie Fitzhugh

Gesu Exterior photo by Abdul R. Sulayman

Villiger Press, 1700 W. Thompson Street, Philadelphia, PA 19121

ISBN 0-9752825-0-6

Library of Congress Control Number: 2004102784

In memory of Rae and Bernard Footlick,
Rebecca and Isaac Cummins, and
Anna and Samuel Footlick

Contents

Preface

For almost four decades I have been writing, speaking, and consulting about American education in its complex and wide-ranging forms from nursery school through graduate school. I have observed its ups and downs, highs and lows—Why Johnny Can't Read, the New Math and the New Physics, The Miseducation of American Teachers, campus protests against the war in Vietnam and in favor of civil rights for African-Americans, desegregated schools, smaller classes, affirmative action, the Education Commission of the States—and written literally thousands of stories about it.

One of those stories exemplified particularly painful times. In 1983, the Gardner Report, *A Nation at Risk*, summarized the condition of our elementary and secondary education in these words: " . . . the educational foundations of our society are presently being eroded by a rising tide of mediocrity that threatens our very future as a Nation and a people. . . . If an unfriendly foreign power had attempted to impose on America the mediocre educational performance that exists today, we might well have viewed it as an act of war."

American education is better than a great many people think it is, bulwarked by a preponderance of hard-working teachers and developing technology. But it is not nearly as good as it ought to be, and most Americans know it. The system is especially ineffective for minority children, who are usually confined to the central parts of the nation's cities. A great many people have proposed solutions to this almost intractable problem, yet as we know from our recent past, most of those solutions don't work. So when something comes along that appears to work, the whole country needs to pay attention.

The Gesu School is something that I believe works, and I am pleased to have had the opportunity to write about it.

This project started with Chris Beck, whom I met several years ago while I was preparing a book about Queens University of Charlotte, of which she is a graduate and trustee. She mentioned to Winston J. Churchill, Jr., the chairman of Gesu's board of trustees, that I might be someone to tell its story as well. After the work began she was always helpful and unflaggingly devoted to the school. None of us could have guessed that as the book was completed Chris would be president of the school.

To identify Win Churchill simply as chairman of the board is like saying Willie Mays was a baseball player. But for his enthusiasm and his understanding of the school's needs and how to fulfill them, Gesu would not have succeeded, perhaps would not exist. Win supported this book in every way, giving of his time and making certain that I met the critical players.

About two years ago I visited Gesu for the first time. Over these many months, I have met the dedicated teachers and staff who make the school function every day; the bright-eyed, well-mannered children who attend and their loyal parents; the extraordinarily loving group of women and men who support it with their volunteer efforts and financial assistance. This school deserves to be widely known.

Allow me to thank some other special people. Father George Bur, S.J., president of Gesu through its first decade of independence, and Sister Ellen Convey, I.H.M., its principal, are the two people most written about in this book, as well they should be. Their intelligence, their warmth, their wit, and their assistance have made my assignment not simply easier, but a pleasure.

Kevin Smith-Fagan, until recently director of development, and Molly de Aguiar, associate director, provided invaluable assistance. Molly gathered a variety of material and answered important questions; she understands needs, and her thoughtful suggestions filled gaps in the work. Pauline Morrison, who runs

Win Churchill's office, solved all kinds of itinerary matters. I much appreciate their efforts.

My thanks as usual go to my computer guru Hugh Tipping, who saves me when he isn't saving international corporations.

And to Ceil Cleveland, the best in-house editor anyone ever had.

Jerrold K. Footlick
Centerport, New York
February 2004

Chapter I

A Beacon Rises

". . . Gesu had always embodied family atmosphere, steeped in the Jesuit tradition—it was almost like a family breaking up."

The darkest day in the history of the Gesu parish—this parish that had served Catholics in the working-class neighborhoods of North Philadelphia for 125 years—occurred on April 2, 1993. On this soft spring day, with tulips blooming in neighborhood parks and lilies in their modest living rooms to remind them of resurrection, the loyal congregants received a message from their bishop, Cardinal Anthony Bevilacqua, telling them that their parish was being *suppressed*, a quaint theological word that meant that it was being wiped out. Here is how the cardinal informed them:

> Dear Brothers and Sisters in Christ of the Parish of the Church of the Gesu:
>
> As you know, our Archdiocese is currently experiencing a nine-year spiritual Renewal. The purpose of the Renewal is to make our local Church stronger and a pleasing gift to our Savior as we celebrate soon the 2000th anniversary of Christ's birth. As part of the Renewal, in conformity with the Archdiocesan Mission Statement, our Archdiocese is committed more than ever to ". . . proclaim to everyone the Good News that Jesus Christ is the Light of the world, who offers to all who follow Him the light of life." . . .
>
> In its efforts to evangelize and serve the People of God, the Archdiocese finds itself confronted today by great challenges. These challenges come from fewer resources and a lower number of priests and religious. Since it is our duty to keep our baptismal promise to assist the Lord in making disciples of all nations, we must at times examine our changed circumstances in order to reinvigorate our mission as Catholics. That is why I initially asked your area to engage in Regional Planning in September of 1991. [After consultation with various groups,] I have reached the decision that I am announcing to you in this letter today.

In order to assure the vitality of the Catholic Church in North Philadelphia, I am closing the parish of the Church of the Gesu and altering the boundaries of Saint Malachy parish to embrace the territory of the parish of the Church of the Gesu. This change will be effective by September, 1993. I wish to thank the clergy, religious and lay staff, especially the members of the Society of Jesus, of the parish of the Church of the Gesu for their dedicated service to the various ministries of the Church at Gesu parish.

I know that the establishment of this new pastoral structure will be challenging and possibly very painful to you. I assure you that I have decided on this course of action only after long and prayerful reflection.

The task of making this transition will be accomplished under the direction of your Regional Vicar. In your area of North Philadelphia, by September, 1993, there will be one parish incorporating the present boundaries of Saint Malachy parish, the Church of the Gesu, and a portion of the territory of the parish of Saint Edward the Confessor. The pastor of the altered parish of Saint Malachy will be Reverend John P. McNamee. By September, 1993, there will be one parish school, one parish pastoral council, and the one parish finance committee. The parish will be located at the present site of Saint Malachy Parish. The school which had been the parochial school at the site of the Gesu parish will continue to be maintained by the Jesuit Fathers and staffed by lay faculty and the Sisters, Servants of the Immaculate Heart of Mary as a private Catholic elementary school.

Our faith teaches us that it is in dying that we are born to eternal life. We know that from the present struggle will come great new life. I deeply appreciate the cooperation that you have given to your pastor during this time of Regional Planning and I ask for your continued loyalty to him. I know that you will offer your support and solidarity to your new parish and pastor.

The Easter season tells us much about the fact that from the experience of death, Jesus gave us victory and new life. I hope that your new parish will be a source of renewed life for you. May the new means of pastoral care and outreach being established in your area bring new vigor to our task of building up the Kingdom of God.

Sincerely yours in Christ,
[signed] Anthony Cardinal Bevilacqua
Archbishop of Philadelphia

So it was done. After nearly two years of meetings and negotiations, anger voiced and silent, tears of rage and anguish, the parishioners of Gesu had lost their struggle for survival. Byron McCook, who had been baptized in the Gesu and grown up to become president of the parish council—a leader like his father before him—said, "I was devastated, very devastated, because Gesu had always embodied family atmosphere, steeped in the Jesuit tradition—it was almost like a family breaking up."

And more than the parishioners would suffer, McCook knew. "It was not only a tremendous loss to those of the Catholic faith who lived in the community, and even those out of the community, but also a tremendous loss to the community of non-Catholics who were ministered to so often by the church itself."

What did survive was a building, the red-bricked, white-columned Church the Gesu with its vast barrel-vaulted ceiling 100 feet high, still in place between the elite St. Joseph's Preparatory School to which the parish had given birth and the tiny homes and shabby vacant lots of a beleaguered North Philadelphia neighborhood.

What also survived, as the cardinal noted, was a school, now to be a private Catholic elementary school "maintained" by the

Jesuit Fathers and "staffed" by lay faculty and the Sisters, Servants of the Immaculate Heart of Mary.

It is now called Gesu School, and it has not only survived but thrived—no, much more than that, risen as a beacon to those who believe that education can succeed in the inner city, no matter the dingy and dangerous surroundings, no matter the hardships for children and teachers.

All it takes are caring teachers and administrators, loyal children and their families, and dedicated friends of all faiths. It is difficult to assemble such a glorious mosaic, but it is not impossible, as Gesu School is proving every day.

Chapter II

Toiler in the Urban Vineyards

"If every kid in Philly had a stable housing situation, education would truly benefit. . . . And there is a good deal of shame in our society about our failures."

George Bur remembers the first time he saw the Gesu neighborhood. His mother's family lived not far away, and his parents frequently brought their family from suburban Abington to visit. Usually they drove, through comfortable streets and Fairmont Park. One day, Bur thinks he was about 10 or 12 years old, he, his brother, and their father boarded a church bus to the city for an outdoor religious service. The bus passed through North Philadelphia, and the wide-eyed boy, looking out the window, witnessed battered houses, littered lots, grown-ups sprawled idly on stoops, and raggedly dressed children playing in the streets. "It was a revelation to me," Father Bur says now. "I suppose I thought then that we ought to do something about it."

The images from that day stayed with him, Father Bur said, and led him to the first of his two notable careers in the Society of Jesus. During his advanced theological studies, he began to work with housing activists in poor and minority sections of Baltimore. After completing his theology preparation, he was expected to return to the teaching of mathematics and physics in a Jesuit prep school. Instead, Bur was allowed to work with another Jesuit in the foundation of a cultural center for black families, part of a broad coalition of community activists and social-service agencies.

"I had little preparation for it, but it was exciting," said Bur, still sounding excited. "We were part of the civil-rights movement as it unfolded in the housing market. We had excellent black mentors, and we provided some of the nitty-gritty research and public-relations skills. The issues were clear, and I felt a certain comfort level in publicly demonstrating from such a clear position. The issues were local and actually involved some constructive engagement—and conversation with the people who were the object of the demonstrating.

The overall result," he said with some pride, "was a change in the market within a few years from widespread exploitation of the black homebuyer to one of growing equity for both black and white buyers." At the same time Bur received his first major political lessons: "What most distressed me was the complicity of the major politicians and big banks in the exploitation."

He also learned—he was not the first Jesuit to discover this—the perils of becoming so involved in the community that he was occasionally unable to offer the cool judgments required in difficult negotiations. He had not learned well enough how to say "no." "There was a time in Baltimore," Bur said, "when I felt so engaged and in a certain sense even trapped by the expanse of the work and the relationships that built up over the years."

Finally it became too much for him, and Bur asked for a change. That is how he was assigned to Philadelphia, the Church of the Gesu, as assistant pastor in 1985 and began his second career. "There were a number of positive features in this change. I could continue to work as a Jesuit in the African-American community. I could be closer to my father who had reached his eighties and was living alone. I could use the pastoral skills that I had built over the years. And I thought I would be using some skills acquired in the area of neighborhood housing."

In fact, the Gesu pastor, Jesuit Father William Perkins, intended to use Bur's housing experience. He asked the new assistant to spend half his time working with a small non-profit group called GRAND, for Girard-Ridge Area Neighborhood Developers, which had begun as a Gesu outreach. Bur was to serve as a consultant to a young, inexperienced African-American woman who had been hired as full-time director.

His first year consisted mainly of trying to understand the politics of the Gesu neighborhood, and he quickly discovered that circumstances were different in many ways from what he had encountered in Baltimore. There was not, first of all, a housing vacuum. More painfully, "The local organizations distrusted the church." Bur could not get comfortable with many of the leaders in the church and the neighborhood; from his perspective, "Some had their own agendas that I couldn't buy into or help with. Others knew exactly what to do and didn't want any more input."

Bur's wry summary of those early months: "A not so politically astute white Catholic priest was trying to compete in a market place with experienced African-Americans who were much more welcomed by the politicians who controlled local housing funds. The days when Gesu parishioners and priests could call some of the political shots had ended with the final days of the [Mayor Frank] Rizzo administration in 1984. And the neighborhood was fast bottoming out."

GRAND tried various tactics. One was to remind the local residents that gentrification—the possibility of losing their neighborhood to white Yuppies—was a real threat. The threat faded, though, because changes in the tax laws and a sharp increase in the crack trade halted the gentrification movement about three blocks away. Some poorer homeowners worried about property taxes, but in general the neighborhood paid relatively low taxes. Some efforts did succeed modestly, for example, a plan for energy conservation. GRAND also owned and managed a few apartment units, which helped a number of residents, but this too was short-lived.

Before long, the GRAND board and its young executive director clashed regularly. Bur tried hard to avoid the conflict, knowing full well it was no-win for him, but was inevitably dragged in. The director was finally fired on issues of financial management, the board took over management directly, and soon the property management accounts were sucked dry.

"Now the properties are vacant and vandalized," Bur said. "To my great sorrow the housing that immediately borders our school is in far worse shape now than it was in 1985."

While Bur was trying to fathom the political tides of North Philadelphia, the parish was, to understate the matter, struggling. It had lost the preponderance of its membership, left with a dedicated but tiny core, largely African-Americans, a handful of whites. Its parish school enrollment had fallen to 200, partly because much of the building was in such disrepair as to be nearly valueless; the very existence of the school seemed threatened by the teetering economics of the congregation. It had almost no operating funds beyond a $100,000 annual subsidy from the archdiocese, which the new Cardinal Bevilacqua was already suggesting would not continue indefinitely. It continued to use a magnificent edifice that it didn't need and cost far too much to maintain.

The popular Father Perkins, who as it turned out had a great many things on his mind, sought desperately to secure the future of his parish. He and lay leaders worked out a plan to shelter all parish programs in the underused school building—worship space, offices, and education. This allowed the parish to abandon the Church of the Gesu structure to St. Joseph's Prep, which was the owner of record and already provided much of its support.

Perkins next prevailed upon the Maryland Province of Jesuits to commit $1 million to renovate the building, only about half of what might eventually be needed, yet a daring start. "This investment was a leap of faith," Bur said, "because there was no guarantee that Gesu would ever be able to support its parish and school mission. Any hard-nosed financial manager would have judged this million-dollar investment in renovations as highly risky."

Then the next shock. With almost no notice, Father Perkins resigned. To marry. Now Bur found himself, in the summer of 1988, pastor of the Church of the Gesu

The school year began with the building under reconstruction, teachers and staff trying to cope with continual interruptions. The dwindling congregation missed Father Perkins, and Bur lacked confidence in his own administrative ability. "It was tough going, opening the school in the middle of major repairs and keeping everything afloat. I was fortunate to have good staff and many supportive people who were good to me even when I failed their expectations."

In the press of these duties, Bur realized that the skills he had developed to deal with housing for the poor, the skills he had expected to contribute in North Philadelphia, were simply going unused. But not, in a way, wasted. "In Baltimore, we Jesuits often had conversations about how we fit into the framework of the Jesuit Province, so heavily invested in education. Actually there were many, many ties. Often the lay people in the housing industry were Jesuit educated, and some even very supportive of our work.

"We thought of ourselves as educators, not only of the housing consumer who came at the issue with almost no understanding, but also of the wider housing community, which did not want to think of itself as exploiting people. So we were educators without a school, but with a center financed by Catholic Charities and with the ability to make headway in the media.

"One thing I did miss in Baltimore was a local church community in which to insert myself. And I certainly found that here. That could have happened, too, with a neighborhood housing endeavor centered in a parish, but, circumstances as they were, the local church and then a local school became the place where I feel most at home."

Then to the question of how one gets from there to here.

"There is no straight line in my own mind from Baltimore housing work to a Philadelphia private Catholic grammar school. It is not as if I knew in 1985 what I would be doing even in 1988. But the straight line does, I think, exist in the framework of the Jesuits. Considerable time is spent by a small staff of Jesuits in determining the place where a man can best use his talents and how we as a group can 'respond to the times.'

"Sometimes they do not find the right place for a man and other times surprise circumstances like a departure from the Society completely befuddle our plans, but I feel as though the system worked in my case. It is a system that at its best can be creative and responsive to people's needs.

"Of course, housing is still a very important issue. If every kid in Philly had a stable housing situation, education would truly benefit. But I cannot think of a week in the past ten years in which articles about the education of our urban children did not appear in the daily paper. And there is a good deal of shame in our society about our failures."

So it was education, not housing, to which Bur would now turn his attention primarily. He also had to try to keep a parish going, and that was not going so well. In 1991, the excruciating two-year process of what the archdiocese called "cluster planning" began. By 1993, George Bur was no longer pastor of a parish; he was president of an independent Catholic elementary school.

No one could be confident at that stage about how the freshly independent school would fare. Yet ten years later, when the Society of Jesus called upon Father Bur to leave Gesu and apply his calm, kind demeanor to a new assignment at St. Joseph's University, the circumstances in this corner of North Philadelphia were much brighter indeed. The road from then to now opened, in that difficult period, because several very good things happened to George Bur and Gesu. They had names: Neil Ver'Schneider, Ellen Convey, Winston J. Churchill, Jr.

In 1989, Father Ver'Schneider, a Jesuit who had been a pastor in Buffalo, New York, decided to give up that responsibility but wanted to continue to work in the African-American community; he passed up opportunities in New York City to become an assistant pastor at Gesu. The next year, Sister Ellen Convey, of the order, Sisters, Servants of the Immaculate Heart of Mary, arrived to become principal of the Gesu School. The next year, Win Churchill arrived to take a look at the roof.

For all the obstacles, the future of the Gesu School somehow seemed more promising than it had in many, many years.

Chapter III

A Very Good Use

"I knew the constituency of the school and had visions that maybe it was not viable—the last thing we need is a cage on an empty building."

For Win Churchill, the beginning was a meeting of the board of trustees of Georgetown University in Washington, where he was chatting with Father James A. Devereux, another member of the board and then the provincial (chief administrator) of the Province of Maryland, Society of Jesus. "Jim said, 'we have this grade school in a building next to your old prep school. We want to put a cage back on the roof of the building, so the kids will have a playground, and maybe you could help. Why don't you go down there and talk to George Bur, the pastor.' I said, sure, I'd be glad to. I called George and made an appointment, and when we saw each other, we realized we had been in the Prep together. He was a year behind me, and we had lost touch."

George Bur took Win Churchill to the roof, which to Churchill looked exactly as it had in 1958 when he graduated from the Prep—brick parapets, tarpaper surface, except now covered with soot "about an inch deep." The roof was bordered by rusty fragments of what had been a fence and had been condemned for school use by city inspectors.

Having seen what was required for the cage, Churchill, whose professional career revolved around money, casually asked to see the school's books. Bur seemed to Churchill a bit embarrassed, "but I said, come on, George," so they sat down to look at the books. "I wanted to know how they were doing on an operating basis," Churchill said, "because Jim Devereux told me that the Jesuits had just put a million dollars into the building to meet the fire code, for sprinklers and stuff. I knew the constituency of the school and had visions that maybe it was not viable—the last thing we need is a cage on an empty building."

At that time, in 1991, the venerable Gesu parish was engaged in the protracted negotiations with the archdiocese of Philadelphia that culminated in its suppression eighteen months later. Bur conceded that the school was losing tens of thousands of dollars annually in its operations, and he didn't know where the money to support it would come from. "George was a pastor, a very good pastor, a great priest, a great head of the school," Churchill said, "but he had never had any kind of fund-raising exposure or desire to do it. And they never had any external sources of funding, other than the archdiocese and what the Jesuits added."

Churchill considered the circumstances and decided to endow a development office for perhaps three years, to see if the school could attract any independent money. "George said, 'Great,'" Churchill remembered, smiling. "What's he got to lose?"

Raising money and putting it to good use is what venture capitalists like Winston J. Churchill, Jr., do for a living. In the case of the Gesu School, he has ventured his own funds and inspired others to join him in a very good use.

Win Churchill knows what it is like not to have a lot of money, and he knows what education can do for an ambitious young person. He also spent formative years observing the degradation that can overwhelm blacks in America and working to alleviate those conditions. So, much that had occurred in his life fitted him for the role he decided to undertake after the serendipitous meeting with his friend Jim Devereux and the reunion with his erstwhile schoolmate George Bur, which was nothing less than to ensure the future of the Gesu School.

The Winston Churchill of this story is no relation, as far as he knows, to his more famous namesake (Winston Leonard Spencer Churchill). His father, also Winston J. Churchill, born in 1910, was probably named after the great Briton in honor of his feats in the Boer War. The senior Winston was born in Philadelphia, the son of a Welsh immigrant who had been a minister, a soldier in the Salvation Army, a part-time actor. He left high school before graduation to work in the mailroom of the Insurance Company of Philadelphia, which after a series of mergers became the international financial giant CIGNA. Blessed with a mind for numbers and calculating skills, he was noticed by senior executives and taken into training as an actuary, eventually working his way to chief of the Philadelphia home office.

Win's mother, Virginia Kelly, was the youngest of eight surviving children in her old-fashioned Irish family; she left school at the age of twelve when her mother died and spent her growing-up years as the housekeeper for her father, a carpenter, and was a surrogate mother to her older siblings. (This Kelly family of Philadelphia was also no known relation to the John Kelly family, he the onetime bricklayer who became a construction-company mogul and had an actress daughter named Grace; there are a lot of Kellys in Philadelphia.)

Virginia's family naturally disapproved of the non-churched Protestant Winston, but they married anyway in 1935, soon had twins, and their son, Winston, Jr., in 1940. The family lived then in a section of Philadelphia called Mayfair, the innermost of a group of ethnic neighborhoods near the northeast corner of the city. Win's earliest memories, though, follow the Churchill's move to West Oak Lane, a neighborhood of tough Irish and Eastern European kids—and tougher nuns who used their rulers freely on the knuckles of recalcitrant boys.

When Win was in 7th grade, his family, like so many others in the transitional neighborhood, moved to the suburbs—"way up in Montgomery County, a big deal to move out of Philadelphia." There he finished grade school, where he performed with almost no effort and was always at the top of his class. Once ready to enter 9th grade, and attempting to emulate his older brother, he applied to take the entrance examination for St. Joseph's Prep. "I remember being absolutely terrified," Churchill said.

The applicants, nearly 1,000 of the brightest Catholic boys from Greater Philadelphia who were to compete for fewer than

200 places, were separated into various classrooms, most of them knowing only a few others, "everyone nervous, chattering." "In comes this more imposing teacher than I had ever seen in my life, in his tweed jacket, and he sits on a corner of a desk, and just by his look imposes silence. He didn't say a word for ten minutes, or it seemed that long. Then he starts to rearrange the groups by pointing his finger, never saying a word, until nobody was sitting with anybody he came in with. This was my first experience with the Prep. I said to myself, 'Oh, this is a new ball game.'"

Win Churchill speaks of the Prep experience with respect for both the academic rigor it demanded and the egalitarian culture it fostered. "My whole life revolved around the Prep." He met boys who are his friends and business associates today. He met Italian boys from South Philly—"sharp dressers, they'd go straight from the Prep, put on their zoot suits, and we'd see them on TV, on 'American Bandstand.'" He discovered rowing and played a season of football. He found that Prep panache opened social doors to Philadelphia's elite Catholic girls schools. Catholic, of course. In his family, "sure not a Protestant girl. I don't think I knew any Protestants then."

In summer Churchill labored on a construction gang, hauling shingles, stirring concrete, pounding nails, to earn tuition money. "We'd start at 7 in the morning when it was cool. Work all day, then I'd come home and sit on the back stoop of our house, unable to move. I couldn't get to the table for dinner. My mother would bring me a bologna sandwich and Kool-Aid, and I'd eat it and go to bed. At that age, it was good to be physically exhausted. I've probably never been fitter in my life."

Churchill got top-of-the-class grades at the Prep, and he had wide-ranging ambitions about college, but his counselors were giving him "heavy guidance, I would say," in the direction of Jesuit colleges, like Georgetown, maybe St. Louis University.

His mother, one of whose uncles, a Jesuit, had been president of Fordham University in New York, was more specific.

"I had this discussion with her, and said, I want to go to Princeton. She said, you're going to go to Fordham. A little later, now I want to go to Penn. You're going to go to Fordham. I want to go to Harvard. You're going to go to Fordham. Then I said, I want to go to Fordham. You made a wise choice, she said. So I went to Fordham."

His father didn't care particularly what school Win attended, as long as he studied to be an engineer. As it happened, Fordham didn't have an engineering major, and since he had excelled in mathematics and physics at the Prep, he became a physics major. This proved a fortuitous choice. Churchill entered not long after the Soviets unleashed Sputnik and invaded Hungary, so the university inherited some of the best Jesuit physicists from all over Europe. He found the atmosphere "highly competitive, and a little terrifying," but extremely stimulating.

Most valuable of all, though, Churchill met a man who became a second father, and the most important intellectual influence of his life. This was the Jesuit scholar Timothy J. Healey, then the academic vice president of Fordham but also a dorm counselor, and a leader who identified the student cream of the crop and drove them to excel in every way. Healey insisted that the pre-meds and physics majors—"he thought we were Luddites, potentially"—take his literature courses and for fun organized the roughest water polo games Churchill had ever known. By his sophomore year, Churchill had earned a place in Fordham's honors program, which allowed the young men to work out their own schedules and essentially opened the whole college to them.

One of the benefits was a junior year abroad. He began with summer French courses—"and mountain climbing"—at LaRochelle, then matriculated under the faculty of science at the University of Paris. The math and physics were strenuous, but to hear Churchill tell it now, most of the rest was *la vie Boheme*. "We had an election among the seven or eight guys going, and I was elected leader, so there was no adult supervision. A Jesuit would come by occasionally to see if we were alive. I would try once in awhile to see if the rest of the group was alive. A couple guys didn't reappear until June."

After boarding with a French family for the first half of the year, he decided to strike out on his own and settled into one of those many small hotels in the *Quartier Latin*, in the rue Racine. Most of the other guests seemed to be attractive young women, but it took him a long time to discover that they were Air France stewardesses. "I was 20 years old and had hard Catholic principles," Churchill said ruefully, "so I never capitalized on the opportunities."

Back home, with the French year having delivered more than enough physics and math credits, he sampled the upper levels of the Fordham curriculum in literature, history, economics, and philosophy. By this time, Churchill found himself drifting away from science. "I was not creative enough to be a great scientist. Quantum mechanics was the edge of my ability. The mundane stuff I could do. I could learn it, I could do well in courses, but I knew I couldn't advance it." He took the law school aptitude test and earned admission to several leading law schools, then, at Healey's urging, applied for and received a Rhodes Scholarship to Oxford University.

During the next two summers, Churchill and a close friend, John Kirby, interned in the civil rights division of the Robert Kennedy Justice Department, under the leadership of Burke Marshall and John Doar. "I worked on the ground in Alabama and Kirby was in Mississippi, basically interviewing witnesses, preparing voting rights cases, county by county. They didn't trust the FBI. I remember that after my first year at Oxford, everybody laughed that I was doing it again. They said, what the hell, you could go to Greece or India. I was going back to Selma."

Like many Americans on a Rhodes Scholarship, Churchill found Oxford "idyllic." Part of the reason—truth be told—is that many of those Americans had already proven, at least to their own satisfaction, their academic chops and considered the fellowship years almost a Byronic grand tour. They worked relatively little their first year and fairly hard their second. They partied hard much of the time, often with English women who found the Yank scholars a tad different from the English men they had grown up with, just as an earlier generation had been taken with Yank soldiers. (Upon returning to Oxford years later for the first reunion ever of Rhodes Scholars, Win stayed, at least part of the time, in his rooms in New College. It was "freezing cold," which is, one might say, part of the charm of olde England.)

Oxford gave Churchill the pleasure of uniting again with his mentor Tim Healey, who spent some months in Campion Hall, the Jesuit house at the university, undertaking post-doctoral research. "Tim loved the women as much as the guys in an intellectual way," Churchill remembered fondly. "He would challenge them. In most cases, they'd never met a priest, a Catholic, a Jesuit, or an American, and he would just blow them away." (Healey went on to become president of Georgetown University, then president of the New York Public Library, before dying at 62 in 1996.)

Churchill ultimately used the Rhodes experience in a special way, writing in 1965, at the age of 25, a novel called *Running In Place*. He concedes that it was largely a *roman a clef*, except, he hastily adds, for the sex. The reader here deserves samples, beginning with this dead-on introduction of a nervous American to the British academic milieu:

> I did learn from one of my neighbors that you started term off by writing a note to your head tutor, informing him that you had come up.

"Dear Mr. Keith-Orange," I write, "I learn from the Worcester Directory that you are the college tutor in medicine and, therefore, I think, my head tutor. Since arriving in Oxford more than a week ago, I have grown rather anxious to begin work. Could I please have your instructions? Respectfully, John Kokonos."

What I should have said was that since arriving in Oxford more than a week ago I had grown tired of packing and unpacking my bags and rearranging my three pieces of furniture. I mean, we'd been told that things might seem rather unstructured but holy Christ.

Keith-Orange's note in reply came several days later . . . "My dear Kokonos," Keith-Orange wrote, "Mrs. Keith-Orange and I should be glad to see you for sherry this afternoon at six. . . ."

I knocked on the door with the heavy door knocker and waited. Who is that tall American messing about with Mrs. Keith-Orange's knocker?

Mrs. Keith-Orange came to the door, opened it and started in like an excited sparrow. "Oh, g-good evening," she said. "You must be one of Hugh's n-new Americans." . . .

I crossed the threshold into a small vestibule and she gave me a glass of sherry from a silver tray near the door. . . . I stood there in the vestibule for a few minutes admiring Keith-Orange's umbrellas and practicing my sherry sipping technique. In due course, Keith-Orange appeared. He had a full, red beard and red hair and he was dressed in an incredibly bulky brown tweed suit. He looked like a flushed red-headed grizzly bear. . . .

"Do you like the sherry?" he asked speculatively.

"Yes," I said. "It's very dry."

"Yes it 'tis."

"But good."

"Yes," he said. "Damned good, actually." He put a match to his pipe and inhaled a tremendous lungful of smoke. . . . "I wanted to have a word with you, though," he said. "Before you go in and get too involved." . . .

He took a couple of puffs on his pipe. "You see, Kokonos," he said, "the first really important thing at Oxford is to get well settled. One must be comfortable before getting down to work. You chaps, you Americans, have particularly to learn that you're not here to do it all in two years. You're here to begin a lifetime of scholarship."

"I hadn't thought about it like that," I said.

"Yes, well, there you have it," he said. "A lot of you people work yourselves silly all through high school and college, trying to get over here, only to spend all your time here hurrying to get finished so that you can get back. It's compulsive, damned compulsive." . . .

The student's grand tour continues on Christmas holiday in Paris:

December was a marvelous month to be in Paris that year. I took a room in a tiny hotel in the rue Racine, [Editor's note: Remember the junior-year-abroad hotel in the rue Racine?] around the corner from the Odeon and the American Library . . . . I went and drank at some of the great cafes while I was there: the Dome, Lilas, the Cluny. . . . Another great thing to do in Paris is to put on a jacket and tie and go for a drink in one of the great hotels, like the George V or the Ritz. After that, you can sit around the lobby reading the newspapers and admiring the women's legs. If you're imaginative enough it's almost as good as going to the Crazy Horse.

The Metro, of course, is great. What you want to use it for is to go to the little neighborhood cinemas in the working class districts of the city when they are showing American westerns dubbed into French. If you sit right on the edge of a

good group and smile a lot they will share their wine and gar-
lic sausage with you and the comments are great.

Even better than the Metro are the buses that run to Etoile
or Montparnasse or the Bois de Boulogne. If you take just one
route a day, ride to the end of the line, have lunch at a neighborhood café nearby, take a walk after lunch and ride back, you
can learn a lot about Paris in three or four weeks.

By the time I left I had learned that if you're going to be
alone somewhere, Paris is not a bad city to be alone in.

Back in the States, Churchill moved on to Yale Law School,
where his classmates included Joe Lieberman, U.S. Senator and
Vice Presidential candidate, and Jeff Greenfield, political opera-
tive and television commentator; and his academic hero was
Guido Calabreze, who taught torts, became dean of the law school,
then a Federal judge. His first job after graduation was at a large,
old-line Philadelphia law firm, Saul, Ewing, Lemrich, where he
quickly gravitated to financial practice, which he attributes to his
understanding of math "and my sort of Welsh interest in money."

After a couple of years, Churchill and another associate persuaded the firm to let them open a pro bono law office in West
Philadelphia. The young lawyers would serve their white-shoe
clients all day, then travel by subway to a storefront office,
where they would spend evenings and weekends taking whatever cases walked through the door. "We were scared," Churchill
remembered, "much more worried than about what we did all
day long." Although they were better prepared in civil law, nine
out of every ten cases were criminal. He learned that there were
a good many bright assistant district attorneys prosecuting
those cases, but he also learned just how cunning the veteran
defense lawyers could be.

Soon after becoming a partner in 1972, Churchill was
assigned by the Saul, Ewing firm to represent one of its major

clients, First Pennsylvania bank, in a class-action suit turning on alleged accounting fraud by a major natural-resources mutual fund. In Denver, surrounded by experienced class-action lawyers who were grabbing plaintiffs catch-as-catch-can, he found himself appointed lead counsel by the Federal judge simply because he had a real client. The case lasted for six years, which, among other things, allowed him to learn to ski, and ended satisfactorily when the fund's insurers, including Lloyd's of London, settled for about $25 million, "a good sum in those days."

Churchill eventually took charge of Saul, Ewing's financial departments and another responsibility he liked better, recruiting associates and summer interns to the firm. "I was finding myself less interested in law practice and more interested in training young people." He also worked on a First Pennsylvania matter again—this time helping save a few hundred million dollars of shareholder value through a public-private bailout as the bank was going belly up.

The transition in Churchill's career came through his work with a merger-and-acquisitions client, Bessemer Securities in New York. Part of a trust established by the steel magnate Henry Phipps in the early 20th century, Bessemer Securities liked to find sleepy, steady companies, invest in them, hire skilled managers to run them, and savor the profits. So intrigued was Churchill that in 1984 he took a leave of absence from his law firm to help manage some of Bessemer's private equity operation.

The Bessemer experience "was how I learned to do this business—that was my training ground," he said. Armed with his share of the assets, Churchill returned to Philadelphia in 1990 to start his own venture capital and private equity operations. They now function through two companies, SCP (originally Safeguard, Churchill, and Plumb; Churchill is the only one of those names now active in the firm), and CIP, for Churchill Investment Partners.

SCP and CIP operate from a modern building in Wayne, Pennsylvania, not far from Valley Forge. (He lives about five miles away in Malvern, the end of the Main Line, in an old French country house, the last and westernmost home designed by the well-known Philadelphia architect Walter Darrow.)

SCP clients are primarily large public pension funds, unions of Pennsylvania teachers and New York police and firefighters among them, for which SCP manages a passive pool of money. (Churchill had once been appointed by Governor Robert Casey of Pennsylvania as chairman of the finance committee of the Public School Employees Retirement System, the largest financial institution in the state.) CIP, the older of the two Churchill operations, is a venture fund; it seeks start-up business opportunities to support with seed money, sometimes bringing in funds of SCP clients.

He credits the famous New York firm of Kohlberg, Kravis & Roberts with "paving the way" for the whole private-equity industry, offering huge incentives on the upside for managers while clients bear most of the losses if they occur. On the other hand, it takes hard work and a set of sophisticated skills to pick the right companies and run them well, and if losses do occur with any regularity the clients are gone. "I learned the power of working with other people's money," Churchill said, "if you can do it successfully."

He also learned, thanks to a lifetime of personal and professional experiences, the value of using other people's money—and his own—to advance the commonweal.

For a business publication, *Fast Company* magazine, Churchill wrote an essay in 2000 called "What's the Best Way to Do Good?" It said in part:

If you do things right, your philanthropic projects begin to build on one another, just as your business projects do. In fact, after awhile, a seamlessness develops between your nonprofit ventures and your business ventures.

We have in our business's portfolio about thirty investments at any given time. Adding nonprofits to those is just a question of how we organize and delegate. We support two schools in impoverished neighborhoods of northern Philadelphia. . . .

Working with these schools is the most natural thing. We treat them exactly the way that we treat fledgling or middle-stage companies. The students are members of our constituency. We feel the same responsibility to them as we do to our portfolio companies, and we make sure that they have a chance to make the most of their lives.

If you're an entrepreneur, you already know how to do venture philanthropy. It's a seamless fit with your business. The next step is just to start doing it. Hemingway said that a writer is somebody who writes. That's just as true with giving back. Pick something that jibes with your values, and begin.

Plainly the Gesu School was such a something. To some, perhaps, this struggling school in this struggling neighborhood might not have seemed a wise investment for a shrewd financier. To hear Win Churchill tell it, though, Gesu amounted to a philanthropic slam-dunk:

"I thought, basically, you have a Catholic school, run by Jesuits and Sisters of the Immaculate Heart of Mary, in the inner-city, the worst neighborhood in Philadelphia, and no Catholic kids, and with a good result. What's not to like? If we can't raise money around this theme, we should hang it up."

Chapter IV

A Leader and a Team

"I like seeing them learn things. I like seeing them getting excited when they know they can do it."

"**I** was the world's worst teacher," Sister Ellen Convey said, remembering her first assignment, at the age of 20, to a parochial school in inner-city Philadelphia. "In my first year, the principal was very ladylike. She would come into my room, and whatever I was doing, she would take over the lesson, and she would say to me, 'Do me a favor and proofread this,' or, 'Do me a favor and add up these.' I didn't realize it at the time, but what she was doing was settling the children down and getting them back into behaving. But she was lovely. She never said anything critical to me."

The second year seemed only marginally better. "I was bringing my class down the steps. There was a retired sister who worked in the office, very hard of hearing, and she had a very gruff tone to her voice, and she wasn't very friendly. She said to me, 'It's so good to see you walking down with your class, instead of chasing after them.'"

The image that came to my mind, hearing those tales, was of Maria, the adorable but occasionally bumfuzzled young nun in *The Sound of Music*. "I learned the hard way, let's say," Sister Ellen recalled. "But it was fun."

It was also a particularly challenging time for this young nun-in-training, hurled into a school in a changing neighborhood of Southwest Philadelphia—a neighborhood of white flight, tense community meetings, racial misunderstandings that sometimes brought physical violence. All this melded with protest against the agonizing war in Vietnam. And protest the young Sister Ellen did, although she emphasized that she "wasn't a leader. We would go and stand in the background."

Perhaps not a leader then, but a leader unmistakably now. In various conversations with teachers at the Gesu School, from a young woman who had been on the job a week to another woman who had taught at the school for nearly three decades, women and men, Catholic and non-Catholic, black and white, I heard tale after tale of respect for their principal, for Sister Ellen's stewardship of Gesu's classrooms and curriculum, and the faculty's trust in her judgment.

Phil Campbell, who taught 6th grade and coached sports, said that Sister Ellen was the reason he came to Gesu and is "still a motivating factor for me staying to this day. In fact I can't think of working for another principal. I don't know that somebody else can live up to my expectations of a principal that Sister Ellen has set for me. My goal is to be a principal some day, and when I think of how to be a principal, I always think of Sister Ellen." (Campbell is now teaching part-time, advanced mathematics classes, while he works toward a doctorate at the University of Pennsylvania.)

Melinda Barno, a feisty 7th grade teacher and math specialist, admires her boss's willingness to support her staff. "I've been in the public schools, where I did student teaching, where the principal was not behind the teacher at all. I have girl friends who teach in the public-school system and complain about that. They say, 'I had a thing with this parent, and my principal sat there agreeing with everything the parent said.'

"My principal doesn't do that. When you're with the parents, she won't put the blame on anyone. Even if I may have done something technically wrong, Sister Ellen will tell you later that you're wrong, but she won't belittle you in front of a parent. She says, 'Here's how you could have done it.' She'll just say, 'OK, woulda, shoulda, coulda, but the bottom line is, we're going to move on.'"

As she considers her present role, leading a group of hard-working, modestly paid teachers through always-challenging, sometimes-frustrating circumstances, Ellen Convey seems a bit surprised that her career developed as it has. A few years ago she thought her life would be more conventional. She grew up in a conventional, suburban, middle-class Catholic home, in

Bristol, Pennsylvania, north of Philadelphia, her father a traffic manager for a trucking company, her mother a homemaker, with enough to do at home raising five children, of whom Ellen was the oldest.

From grammar-school days Ellen admired the nuns of the Congregation of the Sisters, Servants of the Immaculate Heart of Mary (I.H.M.), which is widely known as a teaching community. At 17 she entered the I.H.M. motherhouse, west of the city on the Main Line, beginning a process that the I.H.M. says gives a young woman a sense of participation in the religious life and gives the congregation an opportunity to examine a candidate's potential.

Ellen lived in the convent for three years while taking classes at Immaculata College across the road, then according to plan embarked on her first outside assignment, teaching 4th grade at the Most Blessed Sacrament school at 56th and Chester in Philadelphia. It was here that Ellen was exposed for the first time to the racial tension of the inner-city.

And here, too, she and other young women of the church felt called to join the anti-war protests in Philadelphia. "We were never in any of the big ones, where the Berrigans were," Ellen said, but the priests Daniel and Phillip Berrigan were heroes to many young religious of the time. "We used to read about them, and talk about them—and idolize them."

The brothers Berrigan had become icons to thousands of young people, Catholic and non-Catholic alike. The youngest two of six boys born to a devout Irish-German Catholic family in Minnesota, Dan was ordained a Jesuit and Phil a Josephite in the 1950s. A poet—his volume *Time Without Number* won the Lamont Poetry Award in 1957—Daniel was strongly influenced by the worker-priest movement while studying in France. Among the first Catholic priests to take an open stand in favor of civil rights for black Americans, Philip was one of the original "Freedom Riders" who challenged segregated transportation in the South. The Berrigans attracted national attention in the 1960s for their vigorous leadership in the Vietnam peace movement, although their tactics sometimes caused anguish among friend and foe alike, certainly within the Catholic church

The civil-rights movement, the anti-war campaign, and three and one-half years of teaching and learning in a tough Philadelphia neighborhood changed Ellen Convey. For one thing, she discovered that she was not the world's worst teacher after all. She also completed her Immaculata College degree, then returned to the convent as a "junior professed" to prepare for final vows. In her next assignment as an I.H.M. sister, she learned, more or less, how the other half lives: teaching second grade at a parochial school in the upper-middle-class town of Somerville, New Jersey, where the principal employer was the pharmaceutical firm Smith/Kline/French, the parents were chemists, biologists, and pharmacists, "everybody's going to go to college, and everybody's got everything at home that they need."

Ellen's learning curve continued through four years in Reading, Pennsylvania, not a racially troubled place like inner-city Philadelphia, but a sad town, a victim of changing times, the railroads gone, the coal mines largely picked clean, no new industry moving in, the small-business core dying. A refreshing cultural lesson came with an assignment to Athens, Georgia, home of the University of Georgia and the special brand of Southern friendliness she had never previously been exposed to: her 6th-grade charges responded with "yes, ma'am" and "no, ma'am." "I loved Athens," she recalled. "I thought it was a wonderful place to raise children."

After her two-year sojourn in the soft-spoken South, she returned to the Most Blessed Sacrament School where she had begun her teaching career as a callow 20-year-old. Ellen was different, and Most Blessed Sacrament was different. Back in the early '70s, in a neighborhood that was changing but retained a strong Catholic presence, Most Blessed Sacrament had enrolled children of diverse racial groups in kindergarten through 8th grade, about 2,400 in all, requiring as many as six sections for every grade. Upon her return, the school had one section for each grade, about 200 pupils, all of them African-American.

The new experience helped prepare Ellen Convey for the pivotal event of her professional life: in 1990 she moved a couple of miles crosstown to become principal of Gesu School. Like Most Blessed Sacrament, Gesu had dwindled in the face of white flight and had been serving an almost entirely African-American population since the 1960s. It was using only eight classrooms on the second floor of a deteriorating building, all that was required for an enrollment of about 200.

Still, it was surviving because the parish wanted it to survive. Most of the churches in North Philadelphia, representing Catholic, mainstream Protestant, and a host of small denominations, provided outreach to the community. Some sponsored soup kitchens, others job-placement centers or thrift stores; Gesu helped in a variety of ways but it worked hardest to maintain its school. By the time Ellen arrived, the building was undergoing renovation, thanks largely to a major contribution from the Society of Jesus. Soon the first two floors and part of the third floor could be used for classes. Enrollment was slowly creeping up.

Yet her arrival at Gesu coincided with the archdiocesan examination of how the church could best serve its changing North Philadelphia parishes. As part of the study, administrators downtown asked representatives of the affected parishes to offer their own plans. This led to almost bi-weekly meetings among pastors, school principals, and lay leaders of the parishes over a period of two years. "People got very emotional," Sister Ellen remembered. "They didn't want their churches to close."

When the decision was made, as Sister Ellen describes it, "the cardinal called our superior general at the motherhouse, and basically said to her, 'We're going to close the church. But if you and the Jesuits want to keep the school open, feel free.'"

Nora DeCarlo remembers better than most those wrenching days. One of the two faculty members at Gesu with more than a quarter-century experience, she arrived in 1972 as a 2nd grade teacher, has taught 1st grade, 3rd grade, and 5th grade as well, and is now teaching "the kids of kids I taught." A native of South Philly, and a product of Catholic schools through graduate work at Villanova University, DeCarlo taught in New York's Greenwich Village and New Jersey before deciding to come home to Philadelphia. On the verge of accepting another position, she interviewed at Gesu, "and I just fell in love with the children, and the place, and it was really inner-city, what I was looking for."

DeCarlo watched the enrollment dwindle and the parish disappear, drugs and gangs dominating the neighborhood, the children exposed to violence on television and on their streets. But she has seen a rebirth. "Abandoned houses are getting occupied today," DeCarlo said, and "the parents show respect for the teachers." Most important, her charges are different. "The kids are more active now, with more energy. Years ago they seemed stifled. Now when I ask a question, hands go up. They're not afraid. They like to answer."

DeCarlo attributes these attitudes in part to the "better conditions for learning, a library now, dedicated teachers, supplies, books. It's more comfortable for everyone." Thankful that "God has given me the health, the energy" to keep up with the children, she comes to work about 7 each morning, "sometimes earlier," and leaves about 4:30 in the afternoon, "sometimes later." "Every year is different," she said, but after three decades, one constant: "I love what I'm doing. That hasn't changed. And I thank God for that."

Melinda Barno has seen the world. With a father in the Marine Corps, she grew up in California and North Carolina, traveled in Europe, attended the International School in Nairobi, Kenya, and high school in Panama. She had never been to Philadelphia until she enrolled at Temple University, which she first noticed because of its basketball team; it seemed conveniently located between her mother's family home in New Jersey and her father's service at the Pentagon.

After majoring in elementary education with an early childhood specialization at Temple, Barno accepted a job working with kindergarten-age children at a North Philadelphia YMCA. She first saw Gesu while escorting children to the after-school program and after an interview with Sister Ellen was offered her first teaching job, a 6th grade classroom. Now she teaches Integrated Language Arts and mathematics to 7th and 8th graders, mostly math classes because she enjoys it so much.

Barno finds that she can help the children like math, too, and "if they really enjoy it, they can get it. I do a lot of games." For example, she writes math questions on a beach ball, and the children stand in a circle and toss the ball. Whoever catches the ball answers the problem in the square where his left thumb lands and tosses it to someone else. "This year in 8th grade I had some of last year's 7th graders, and while we were getting to know each other one of the girls yelled, 'Can we play with the ball?'"

About the same age as some of the young mothers at Gesu, and African-American like them, Barno is not sympathetic when she observes a lack of responsibility. "I asked the mother of one kid with a problem to see me in the morning when he came to school. She said, 'I don't have time to see you. I have two jobs.' I said, 'You don't have time? You had time to have him. If you don't raise him, the world will raise him, and you don't want the world to raise him.' There's always an excuse."

Barno insists she is not unsympathetic about the difficulties of living in the inner city. "My grandparents lived in the projects in Newark. I'm not oblivious to it. I understand it, I just didn't grow up in it. I know these kids have a lot to deal with. Some of them haven't seen their dads in so long." North Philly, she realizes, is a far cry from how she was raised in a peripatetic Marine Corps family. "Responsibility is the hardest thing to teach unless you from the very beginning have been taught to be responsible. I was always taught to be responsible. If something was wrong, I knew there was a price.

"Every place I lived, my mom became very good friends with my teacher. I didn't know this until 5th grade when the teacher called me by the name only my family used. My mom didn't play when it came to school. What you bring to school is what you bring from home."

Outgoing, enthusiastic, Barno is tough-minded about what she wants. She once lived in North Philadelphia but prefers the suburbs where she now lives. "I like inner-city kids but I'm not a city person. I like the suburban life."

Since Barno seemed exactly the kind of person the Philadelphia public schools would want in a classroom, I asked her why she stayed with Gesu. As with many of the other teachers, her answer said quite a lot about Sister Ellen. "I get asked that question all the time. Yes, I could go to the public schools and make twice as much money, but I would have more headaches. The class size is good. And Sister Ellen is a wonderful principal. If an emergency comes up, she is very flexible.

"My grandfather passed away, and my mom called me in the middle of the day. Most places, you've got to get things together, have to get this and that done. Sister Ellen said, 'Just go and don't come back until everything's taken care of. We'll figure out whatever it is you're doing, we'll pick up on it and work it out.'"

Teaching kindergarten at Gesu was Laura Ann Hood's first job out of college, class of 2001 at Widener University in Chester, Pennsylvania, psychology major and certified in early childhood education. It was not her introduction to Catholic primary education, however. Raised in a comfortable Lutheran family in Northeast Philadelphia, she attended a Catholic elementary school because her mother thought it offered the best education around, then passed the strenuous test for enrollment at Philadelphia's fabled Central High School.

While circulating resumes during her senior year at Widener, ruling out only the Philadelphia public school system—"out of the question, too many problems, I didn't want to deal with that"—Hood heard from the mother of a good friend about Gesu. When she arrived for an interview, "the thing that made me the most nervous was, of course, the neighborhood. I had gone from nice suburban St. Dominic's to Central, which was a culture shock anyway. I got used to it in four years, then in college I was back in a pretty suburban campus. So getting into this was, you know, a little scary. It's the idea that it's North Philly. But you get over that, and now I don't think anything of it. I park right on the street. In fact, if I pull up far enough, I can look out my window and see my car. So I feel very safe."

Gesu presented challenges, Hood knew, yet it offered a clear chance of success. "This school has everything that I wanted. I know how much of a need there is for inner-city children, but I couldn't face feeling like a failure in the Philadelphia school district. I still get to work with disadvantaged kids, challenged kids, inner-city kids, in this sort of setting—I can still feel like I'm making a difference and helping them—but without all the hassles."

When Laura Ann and I first spoke, she had worked at Gesu for a month and was in her first week of classes, but she had already undergone one of the perils of a kindergarten teacher: a five-year-old's tears. "This morning a boy threw himself under a desk and started to cry. I am a sucker for kids. I can't see anybody cry. I want them to be independent, but I can't turn away anybody who's crying, who needs a hug. They need to know that I'm going to be there, that I am going to love them all, and take care of them when they're sad. So I picked him up off the floor, held him, and said, 'You can do this. I know it's hard, but you did it before. I'm proud of you.' I put him down, and he picked up his school bag and got started."

Hood had prepared her first curriculum plan—beginning sounds, introducing the children to the "letter people," starting their math with measures of time and money and how they grow, starting science with the weather. "I feel good," she said about the first day with all the children present. "I feel like we spent a lot of time going to the bathroom and washing our hands—going to the bathroom with twenty-five kids is a half-hour deal—but it takes time to get our routines down."

She also liked the atmosphere. "When you come in the morning, everyone is pleasant. People stop by my room: 'Do you need anything?' 'How are you?'" Hood knows she could make more money elsewhere, teaching in public schools or in another vocation. "If I wanted to make more money, I would have been a doctor. Originally I thought I would work here a couple of years, then move out of the city. But I'm happy here, to stay as long as they'll have me. It's everything I want, the best of all my worlds that I was thinking about."

Laura Weatherly has been committed to Catholicism and to Catholic education for as long as she can remember; her commitment to Gesu is more recent but no less firm. The product of Catholic schools from kindergarten through college—her undergraduate degree is in history and education—she earned a master's degree in theology and began teaching at a Catholic school in her native Chester, Pennsylvania. Before long she was director of religious education for her parish, but it was suppressed in 1993 at the same time as Gesu.

Weatherly arrived at Gesu in 1996, bringing with her twin grandnieces, her sister's grandchildren, whom she is raising. "The streets have my niece now," she said, not elaborating on an unpleasant subject, "and I have the children." Two years later she was offered the principalship at nearby St. Malachy's parish, but after four years there decided the administrative routine was too much. In 2002, she returned to Gesu as an 8th-grade teacher.

Even when Weatherly moved to St. Malachy's, and even though she still lives a considerable distance away in Chester, she kept her nieces at Gesu. "I knew I could leave them here and they would be taken care of, not only academically but spiritually and physically taken care of, that during the day, when they came into this building, I didn't have to worry about them. There were so many people here who were looking out for them."

The 8th-grade curriculum, infused with issues of morality, is particularly important to the deeply religious Weatherly. "I love teaching my faith," she said. "I love the church, I love being involved with the church, I love doing the things I do with the church." Might she have become a nun? "Why I didn't, in all honesty, was that you never saw an African-American nun, even in the Catholic school system."

Phil Campbell, product of a middle-class Catholic family, attended Catholic schools all his life, earning an undergraduate degree at Villanova University, teaching credentials from Cabrini College, and a master's degree from St. Joseph's University. After completing his student teaching in the fall of 1997 and interviewing with the Philadelphia Catholic school system, he planned to spend a few months relaxing, working as a waiter or bartender, until the following fall. Unexpectedly, at mid-year, Gesu needed a new 6th grade teacher so Sister Ellen called the archdiocesan office, which gave her Campbell's name.

"Sister Ellen called me at 1:30 in the afternoon and asked if I would like to come in and talk. I said, when should I come. She said, how's 2 o'clock. Anyway, I came in the next morning at 9, Sister and I talked for a half-hour, and she showed me around. I met teachers and saw the kids. She gave me basically fifteen minutes on all the reasons why I wouldn't want to work here, percentage of non-Catholics, single-parent families, all of that. By 10:15 she had offered me the job, and I had accepted it. I felt 'right' in the building. It felt like a place where I wanted to be and needed to be."

Was it the place or his admiration for Ellen that kept him at Gesu? "Well, the kids are absolutely the principal reason that I have stayed. I hear a lot [from my friends], 'What is it like teaching those kids?' I say, 'Those kids are just like your kids, because kids are kids.' Year after year, you see kids coming up and kids who've gone through your class. You want to see what's going to happen next.

"Part of the reason with the kids is that so many people in their lives are transient people, here today and gone tomorrow. They may see them for a month at a time, then they're gone for four months. I want the kids to know that there's going to be some sense of stability—when they come back in September, Mr. Campbell is going to be there." So even as Campbell embarked on his doctoral program in educational leadership at Penn, he committed to continue parttime at Gesu, teaching advanced math courses to 5th through 8th graders.

"I know that financially I'm going to have to move someday," he said. "I'm a single man now, and I'm making enough money to cover my bills, enough money to survive. As far as planning for the future, supporting a family, barring some major financial change here I don't know. I probably would love to stay here forever, but . . . "

It clearly requires special circumstances and dedication for teachers to work at Gesu because the pay scale is a significant detriment. The school has attempted to become more competitive with the Philadelphia public-school system by offering raises of 6 to 8% over the last several years, but it has a long way to go. Gesu's starting salary is just over $25,000 annually, one-third lower than the Philadelphia system; the median is about $30,000 and the highest salary is in the mid $40,000's.

Pension benefits are skimpy and medical benefits apply for the individual, not a family. The school does offer financial supplements for additional work, in the after-school or summer programs or for certain special projects, and some teachers also work part-time at libraries or recreation centers. A teacher might add typically $3,000 annually or as much as $10,000 with a heavy extra load.

Teachers are recruited in a variety of ways, but most of them come soon after college graduation, either through relationships with the school or with trustees; some transfer from other Catholic schools in the area. As of 2002-3, only one had ever been a full-time public-school teacher and only the principal Sister Ellen and the counselor Sister Patricia McGrenra are nuns.

Sister Pat, as she is known to all, sees a faculty remarkably more cohesive than when she arrived at Gesu nearly a decade ago. Too many teachers then appeared unwilling to pitch in to save the school, uncooperative to the point of divisive, she said: "it was a real struggle." Those people are gone, replaced by faculty "who are on board for each other." The attitudinal change became obvious to Sister Pat a couple of years ago in a volunteer faculty meeting devoted to assessing strengths and weaknesses, during which the teachers agreed to meet on their own time over the summer to plan for the next school year.

"It was surprising—no, it wasn't surprising—how many came voluntarily during the summer. We worked on things that were for the good of the kids at all grade levels. The teachers will do extra activities, they'll tutor after school, help each other out on different projects and don't feel the least bit intimidated about asking [for help.] If someone is delayed in traffic coming to school, someone else will take their line, get the kids in the room. [Experienced teachers] mentor new teachers as they come in. They feel they are here for the good of the children. That's our mission, what we're about."

Sister Ellen is still recruiting and shaping a dedicated faculty at Gesu, but she wants her next service, whenever or wherever, to be in the classroom. "I really love teaching," she said. Her opportunities to teach these days are limited to substituting, "but when my time here is done, I'm not going to be an administrator. I'm going to go back in the classroom."

One reason, she explained, is that a principal is forced to spend too much of her time dealing with adults. "I like the kids," Ellen said. "I like the personal relationships you get with the kids. You get to know them better as a teacher than as a principal. I like seeing them learn things. I like seeing them getting excited when they know they can do it." That's why she especially likes the primary grades, where "once they realize they can read, they are so much fun. It's just fun.

"I think kids are not difficult. I know you can never reach 100% of every child; there are difficult cases," Ellen said. But she believes that teachers cause problems for themselves by not arranging a classroom so that children learn to respond appropriately. The challenge, she said, is to make the classroom work—to make it fun—in such a way that the children want to learn. She has not forgotten, however, the importance of classroom control that plagued her in her earliest professional days. A teacher must also make certain that the children "don't give you grief," that they "are not disrespectful."

It seems extremely unlikely that anyone in the Gesu building would be disrespectful to Sister Ellen. Not long ago, a second grader misbehaved enough that the teacher sent her off to the principal's office. As it happened, Ellen was away at the time, and the anxious, tearful child instead faced Sister Pat. Summoning her best counseling skills to calm the little girl, Sister Pat told her to look for the bright side: "Tell me something you are grateful for." Looking up sweetly, the child responded, "I am grateful that Sister Ellen isn't here."

Chapter V

Boys Here, Girls There

"The responsibility for teaching young African-American males is to show up."

Of the number of things we know about Gesu, here are two: First, this school, because of its independence, is free from bureaucratic molasses and can act rapidly to solve academic or social problems and improve the curriculum. Second, the academic leadership is imaginative and flexible, starting with the principal, Sister Ellen, whose judgments are supported by the president, and by the board of trustees, a group willing to take action when conditions demand action.

Gesu's imagination and flexibility is one of the most appealing qualities about the school to its faculty. "Our administration is extremely supportive," said Chris Harris, who teaches 4th grade. "You have an idea, you throw it out there, they'll hear you out. They look at the safety aspects first, and if that's all right, they say, 'Go for it. Try it. Keep us posted.' As a teacher you love that. You love that professional freedom."

Two innovations demonstrate Gesu at its best. One is the single-gender program. The other is the writing program (described in the following chapter).

Gesu's decision to initiate single-gender education in the 3rd, 4th, and 5th grades exemplifies disciplined action in response to a perceived need. "The problem was," Sister Ellen said, "years ago we were graduating classes of twelve girls and six boys. We were just not holding on to the boys; some were sent out for discipline reasons, others were flunking out."

A group of faculty, with Father Neil as chairman, set out to look for answers and discovered an African-American scholar in Chicago whose studies seemed to trace parallels to the Gesu experience: African-American males began to turn off as early as the 4th grade, not doing their homework, sitting in the back of the classroom, allowing girls to take charge of class participation. "That was easy for us to believe," Ellen said.

Gesu's solution was to try to catch the syndrome a year earlier, in 3rd grade, and continue single-sex classes for three years.

"The smartest person in the room had to be a boy, because they're all boys," Ellen said. "Then we put a role model, a good, strong, male role model, with them most of the day; their home-room and major academic teacher would be a male"—while allowing the boys to have a female teacher and the girls a male teacher for a single class a day.

One of those role models is Chris Harris, himself African-American, who believes the fundamental requirement of his job can be stated simply. "The responsibility for teaching young African-American males is to show up. To show up every day. To be dependable. We are allowed to take off personal days sometimes, but I don't want to do that. I think if I take off those days, I would let my boys down because they look forward to seeing me every day." The reliability of the black male teachers, he said, inspires the boys, who are seldom absent. "They come every day. Sometimes they are late, but they come every day. They feel a responsibility just to be there."

H. L. Ratliff, who directs mentoring programs both at Gesu and nearby St. Joseph's Prep while coaching the Gesu choir as well, also feels keenly his responsibilities as a role model. "One of the things that is unusual about Gesu is the number of male teachers who are at an elementary school; at many grade schools you do not see that," said Ratliff, who is also African-American. "What's good is that when you put all the men together, we show a spectrum of differences, age-wise, interest-wise, black and white. The students see that we all have our strengths, our focuses, and although we are certainly different from one another, we work well together."

An example: "I'm one of the few people who wears a suit and tie and pressed shirt every day. That's not to make a statement, aside from, that's just H. L. Ratliff, that's what he does. The gym teacher wears sweats because he's the gym teacher. But we get along really well. I think it's seeing those role models in different places, who have made contributions to the school in different ways, that is the real gift for the students."

Beyond the clear importance of role models, Gesu has found that single-gender classes allow the children to focus academically. "Those are the grades where you get the basic skills," Ellen said. "You get your times tables, and if you don't get them there, the rest of your math is lost. They learn to write paragraphs, to make stories. They get all the basic ingredients they need for high-level subjects. And the kids were getting it, immediately. It was great."

Harris measures how well the kids are getting it by their enthusiasm. "I say, 'take out your math books,' and they say, 'yea, math. I want to do division today.' That's when I know it's working. They're taking an interest in what they're doing. They want to learn.

"I say, 'go home and play school. Practice your work. Pretend you're the teacher, and teach to whomever. Or test yourself.' Little things like that. And the next morning, a boy will come in and say, 'I played school. I got all my math right.' They're motivated. That's half of education."

Inevitably, the success of Gesu's single-gender program has led to calls to expand it, perhaps to the 6th grade, possibly through the 8th. Most of the teachers, seeing something that plainly works, are all for it, but the principal is reluctant.

Ellen contends that by the 6th grade today's children are already into adolescence—"heavy, big-time"—and want social intercourse with the opposite sex. In addition, groups that have been together for three years sometime create their own social problems—cliques that began in 3rd grade, among girls in particular, probably should be broken up, "giving everyone a fresh start." Finally, the boys who by then have three years of confidence-building experience don't need the single-gender classroom as much. The principal concedes, though, that extension at least to 6th grade is "under passive-active consideration" every year.

Harris agrees that the single-gender plan should be maintained only in the "pre-adolescent" years of 3rd, 4th, and 5th grades. He finds that the 4th grade boys "talk about boys' stuff" and are "not pre-occupied with the other sex." Yet they do begin to notice the relationship between the sexes. Many of these boys are being raised by their mothers, and they pay attention, if their mother brings a man home, to "how women and men interact with one another."

Harris believes that "young African-American males have trouble relating to other African-American males," based on tensions in their homes and neighborhoods. "Sometimes they talk to me as if I'm some guy on the street," he said. "I say, 'you don't speak to me or any teacher that way'—I stress that a lot. Their doing that, right there, is showing me that 'I don't have a lot of males around my house, and when I do have males coming around, like my mother's boy friend, I resent him, because he takes time away from me and my mom.' They see the male not as someone to look up to but someone who is not respected, who doesn't respect their well-being."

The opportunity that Gesu, as an independent school, has to experiment is underlined by a similar effort at a Philadelphia public school. There, a principal, sensing the special problems of African-American boys, set up a single-gender 1st grade class with a male teacher; in this case, the teacher moved up with the boys as they advanced in grades. Observing the program in its early stages, teachers and parents thought it was helping the boys, but before long the school was accused of sex discrimination so the experiment had to be abandoned.

Gesu's single-gender program became the subject of a research project conducted by Gail Avicolli, who was then a regional director for the Office of Catholic Education in Philadelphia, serving as academic supervisor for one-third of the 212 schools in the archdiocese's five counties. Avicolli, who grew up in South Philadelphia and began her career as a teacher and principal, visited dozens of Catholic schools, offering strategies to the teachers and helping them find outside resources. Her territory was "very much the inner city," radiating from the old ethnic "river wards" downtown to North Philly and the city's northwestern boundary (Gesu would have been part of this territory if it were still a parish school).

After meeting Sister Ellen at a Catholic school principals meeting and "bonding with her immediately," Avicolli won her cooperation and Father Bur's to make Gesu the centerpiece of her doctoral dissertation at Immaculata University. It was titled, *Single-Gender Education: Impact on Fostering Self-Esteem and Academic Behaviors.*

(Gesu is not named in the dissertation, but everyone concerned knew the purpose of Avicolli's research and the school in the project is identified this way: "The site of this study was Urban Inner City School located in the vicinity of a private, Catholic high school. Urban Inner City School, an independent Catholic elementary school, educates 400 children from pre-kindergarten through eighth grade. Founded in 1879 by the Jesuits . . . since 1960 Urban Inner City School has educated two generations of African-American youngsters in a neighborhood under increasing economic and social pressure. . . . ")

Avicolli's previous research indicated that the academic work of boys dropped off sharply after the 2nd grade, that even boys who had done honors work in the first two grades succumbed. In the Gesu study, both boys and girls said they "felt special" in single-gender classes and boys especially were not as likely to be distracted from their class work. The children appeared "to feel more comfortable taking risks with answers" and "felt better able to handle the ups and downs of their own education." Avicolli found that the program won support not only from teachers and students but also the enthusiastic approval of parents.

Combining her study of the literature with surveys, interviews, and personal observation, Avicolli concluded "that single-gender classes had a positive impact on fostering the self-esteem and academic behaviors of the participating students. This alternative group strategy could be invaluable for elementary and middle-school teachers, students, and parents who are endeavoring to improve students' self-concept, academic behaviors, and self-discipline."

I asked Avicolli how Gesu compared to the sixty-seven parish schools she visited regularly. She responded that a handful of them were in a class with Gesu academically, while observing that the environment at Gesu made it very special. "When I walk in Gesu, I feel like I belong here. I feel very welcome. I can go to the office, to the ladies room, to the lunch room, stop and talk to Father Bur, can go into classrooms. If I can do that as a visitor, then what I say to you is that this school is creating a warm, welcoming environment."

Until she met Sister Ellen, Avicolli had no contact with Gesu. But the more she learned about the school the better she liked it. "The whole package that you would need for a successful student is here. The opportunities are here—all the pieces are in place, the support for individual academic differences, the textbooks, the paper, the cleanliness, the health services, the counseling, the follow-through. Sister has a washing machine here, and the children's things are washed if they're not clean. There isn't one part of their social, emotional, religious, or academic needs that is not addressed.

"They're providing a truly academic atmosphere for the children—it's very clear that there is a strong academic thrust—but it's very clear that this is a school that is going to treat you like family. If you're having a situation, happy or sad, the needs are going to be met as best as possible."

The mutual respect grew strong enough that Avicolli was invited to join the board of trustees (her term recently ended), to which she brought the perspective of a professional educator. "I felt privileged to be a trustee. I feel like we're really touching the future. We're making a difference. Perhaps this model might be something that other people could look at, to ensure a quality education for inner-city children. There's hope here. There's life and there's a future.

"There are problems with the public schools, problems that our pastors are having with the parishes. All those things are iffy. This isn't. This is a for-sure thing. Whenever we try to look outside the box at what might happen in the future, Gesu is a model of what could happen."

Assessing the single-gender effort herself, Sister Ellen reaches her usual pragmatic conclusion. "What we were looking for was to maintain graduates, and we have," Ellen said. "We now don't lose any more boys than is normal. It's been probably the most successful thing we've ever done."

Chapter VI

Telling Their Stories

"Never complete things you know you'll regret
never put off things you know you'll forget."
From a poem by Melissa Williams

Sister Ellen was embarrassed. She had recommended one of Gesu's brightest graduates to a prestigious Main Line academy, and the girl was declined admission. "I knew this girl should go there, and I knew she could get a scholarship," Ellen said. When she didn't, "I called the admissions officer, and said, 'Why didn't you accept her?' and she said, 'Her writing is too shallow.'"

Ellen can laugh now about her first reaction: "I was, like, what 13-year-old's writing isn't—they're all shallow." That is about as much annoyance as she is willing to express openly. But she got the message. "It made me realize that there was a flaw. We were weak in that area of education."

From that experience came the most consequential academic variation from the standard Catholic school curriculum—a forceful writing program, begun in the fall of 1999. Gesu started with a part-time teacher working with about a dozen of the top students in both the 7th and 8th grades. Before long, these children were producing work that Ellen called "unbelievable—unbelievable what happened with the writing program."

Here are a few samples from 1999 and 2000:

The Greatest Gift of All
Melissa Williams, 7th Grade

Death is the greatest gift of all because it's not too big and
it's not too small
cause when you return to the heavens above
God will welcome you with a gift of love.
In life you did the best you could
and your reward came like it should.
Satan tempted you but you turned away
and now your time is here today.
You knew if you sinned you'd dearly pay
and spend eternity in a cruel way.
Read this poem with pride and joy
but here are some things you should avoid.

People who talk a lot don't make good friends.
First loves never seem to end.
Save yourself for the person you love.
Guys get no "pigeons" and girls get no "scrubs."
Never rush into things, take your sweet time
cause after it's done you might change your mind
Never put down people, you'll need them in life
never just guess things, they won't turn out right.
Never complete things you know you'll regret
never put off things you know you'll forget.
Follow these rules and maybe it will be,
when you die heaven you'll see.

What's Wrong with This Picture?
David Still, 7th Grade

Once upon a time there was a boy named Chris. He went to Multi-Racial High School. He had a lot of friends there and all of them were black. All different races went to this school, which caused some problems. Whites only hung out with whites, blacks hung out with blacks, and Chinese only hung out with Chinese.

One beautiful fall day, the seniors were outside playing in the school yard. Chris saw a beautiful girl by the name of Jackie. Chris said to his friends, "What do you think about her? Does she look all right?"

His friends said, "Yeah, but one problem. She's white."

Chris said, "And what does that matter? Girls are girls, and they will always be girls."

His friends said, "You're trippin'. You're only supposed to stick with your own race."

Another friend said, "I always knew you had jungle fever."

Chris said, "If y'all going to be that way, I choose y'all."

But Chris began to change his mind. Every day after that, he started to talk to her more and more. One day Chris's friends saw him talking to Jackie. They said, "Hold up."

Chris said, "I'm talkin', can't you see, and stop bein' rude."

His friends said, "We are not your friends anymore."

Chris said, "'Bye. What are you still standing here for?"

They walked away. Chris said, "Do you want me to take you to class?"

Jackie said, "Okay, why not?"

Chris and Jackie started dating and Chris never spoke to his friends again. Chris learned that friends like that are no good.

After Awhile
Kristen McCook, 7th Grade

After awhile
The moon stops glowing
And the sun will finally shine.
After awhile
You put the pieces back together
And straighten out your mind.
After awhile
A new relationship occurs and now you shine

The Kid in Blue
Turquoise Sanders, 6th Grade

September 3 was the first day of school; everyone was happy to go back except Boota. He was in the fifth grade. He did not like his name because everyone at his last school always teased him. This year Boota did not want to go back to school because he was afraid everyone was going to tease him.

"Boota, Boota, get up," his brother called, shaking him so he could get up.

His brother's name was Scooter. Everyone in his family had funny names. Scooter liked his name. Scooter and Boota are totally different from each other.

Scooter's not good in sports. Boota is good in sports. Scooter wears glasses. Boota does not. One thing that they do have in common is that neither of them has friends.

That morning after Boota got washed and dressed he went downstairs for breakfast. "Are you ready for school today, Boota?" his father asked putting a piece of bacon on the floor for their dog, Rat.

"No," Boota answered with a pout on his face. His father knew why he was not ready for school, so he didn't bother asking why.

When Boota got to school he was afraid to go in his class, but he had no choice. As he walked in he heard a voice from behind him asking, "What's your name?"

Boota turned, looked at him and didn't answer. "I said, 'What's your name?'" the boy asked again.

This time Boota answered, but he didn't answer the boy's question. He asked, "What's your name?"

"Joe," the boy answered.

Boota walked away as far as he could so Joe wouldn't ask him his name again.

Boota looked around for his name on the desks and sat down when he saw his name. He looked at the people around him and their names. He noticed that two people were waving to him and were whispering, "What's your name?"

Boota didn't answer.

Finally, the teacher said, "Good morning, class.

Today we have three new students. Would all three of you come up here, please?"

They all came up. "Would you tell everyone your names at recess?" their teacher asked.

At recess when someone asked Boota his name, he said, "My name is the Kid in Blue."

Everyone looked at him as if he was crazy. The teacher didn't say anything because she knew his problems.

That day at recess, everyone was picking teams for basketball. "I pick the Kid in Blue," one boy said.

From that day on, everyone called him the Kid in Blue, even the teacher.

One day during class, the principal called on the loud speaker and said, "Could I please see Boota for a minute?"

Boota walked out and went to the principal's office.

That day at recess, like always, everyone was picking teams for basketball. "I pick Boota," one boy said.

For a minute, Boota was in shock. He couldn't believe that no one was laughing at his name.

From that day on, everyone called him Boota without any problems.

The Tenth Street Rescue
Kyle M. Carney, 7th Grade

Little Joey was a regular boy like every other boy in town. He was not, though, in the eyes of the boys on Tenth Street. They hated his guts. Every day when Joey was on his newspaper route, they would throw eggs at him, spit on him and take his newspapers from him—anything, you name it. They saw Joey as a little squirt who loved school, loved reading books, loved homework, and enjoyed chores. Since they didn't like any of those things,

58

they decided to pick in him.

Joey never said anything to hurt them, he just did what he did, which was nothing in the eyes of the Tenth Street boys.

Joey wondered why they always picked on him.

One cloudy insipid day, Joey had nothing to do. He read all of his books, did all of his chores and completed all of his homework. But, Joey always knew what to do in these kinds of situations. He decided to go to the huge arcade on Sixth Third Street. He didn't want to bother his parents, so he went in the house and got a token from his room. Joey rode the bus because he likes to see where he's going.

As he entered the big blue doors of the bus, he felt like there was going to be an amazing change in his life.

When he got to the arcade, he felt so happy. (Besides reading and doing chores, he loved to play the arcade games.) As he entered the huge arcade, he saw so many colors, so many people, and most of all, so many games. This made him feel like a little seven-year-old entering an amusement park.

The arcade was color coded (blue is for racing games, etc.). Joey went over to the red section to read about the different game contests. Joey loved game contests, because he was so good at them. Playing against Joey is like a turtle racing a cheetah. He decided to enter the "Ninja Tigers" contest. It's a fighting game where the player battles against other people until the game shuts down. When the player turns it on again, the score determines the lucky winner of the game. If you win, you get $60,000 in cash. Wow! Now that's the kind of contest for Joey.

Two days later, Joey entered the contest and won. He never told anyone about it, not even his dearly beloved parents. He didn't spend a dime of the winnings. He just put it in a jar under his bed and went to sleep.

Joey didn't feel right having all that money for himself. He wanted to give it to charity or help someone. He simply wanted to make a change.

The next day, when Joey woke up from a good night's sleep, he heard a lot of noise coming from outside his window. This was weird, because it was such a peaceful town. So he took off his red pajamas, jumped out of bed, hurtled down the stairs, and ran outside to see where the noise was coming from. The noise was coming from Tenth Street. Joey felt a pain in his stomach, that type of pain you get when you're going up, up and up. He was afraid he was going to get beat up, but something inside him told him to keep on walking.

As he arrived on the scene, he saw three women who were the mothers of the Tenth Street boys. Joey was shocked by the fact that those ignorant boys even had mothers. He was still scared, so he kind of eased over to them. They were crying so loudly that the whole town might have heard them. Still scared, he asked them what was wrong. They told him that they haven't been paying their bills and if they didn't come up with $20,000 each they were going to be forced into a shelter. They didn't want that kind of life, so they cried and cried.

Joey ran home and got his $60,000 and was back in a flash. He told them, if he gave them the money, would they make their sons stop picking on him? They agreed. He gave them $20,000 each and gave them a big hug. They were jumping and shouting. They were just so happy.

The next day was a normal day for Joey. He rose out of bed, put his clothes on and went on his paper route. When he got back home, the Tenth Street boys were waiting for him on his steps. They had gifts, money and cards. They were jumping and shouting.

All day they were cheering for Joey, thanking him, and buying him gifts. They even gave him a nickname: "King Joey."

The moral of the story is not to make fun of or pick on somebody, because you just might need them one day.

*   *   *

Under a grant from Backe Communications, the special writing program has expanded to four days a week for students in grades 4 through 8 and was for several years the only place in the Gesu curriculum where children are "tracked" or separated by ability. (An advanced mathematics program, begun in the fall of 2003, now also tracks students.) The writing teacher, Eileen Erwin, works with the top half of each class, while the home room teacher offers writing to the other children. The division of labor is practical, Sister Ellen explained: "It's hard to teach writing to twenty kids at one time. You need to have conferences as a writer, you really need time one on one."

Obviously the children notice who works with whom, but Ellen believes they have become accustomed to the arrangement. The key to the children's attitude is the home room teacher; if the teacher were to treat the less-skilled writers with relatively less respect, the tracking plainly wouldn't work. But the home room teachers work in tandem with the writing specialist—that is, children in both groups will be writing a narrative poem at the same time or an autobiography—and if they insist on conscientious writing, everyone can improve. "Our writing's excellent," Sister Ellen said with some pride. Certainly the evidence is there.

Eileen Erwin's presence is one more example of the mystical pull that Gesu exerts or its simple good fortune, or some combination. Erwin was completing a Ph.D. in urban education at

Temple University, living on campus, and looking for a teaching opportunity at a school within walking distance, preferably Catholic. "When I learned the unique history of [Gesu] and learned about the writing program, I was thrilled," she said. "It was perfect to be writing a dissertation about teaching writing in urban schools and doing just that."

Like almost everyone who happens upon Gesu, Erwin said immediately, "It really feels like a family here." Beyond that, in her own specialty, she found well-tended ground. "I have been stunned by the writing skills of students at this school. To see raw creativity and talent is a blessing."

The children work in many genres, including poetry, plays, essays, and short stories. Here are samples from two of the younger children in Erwin's first classes, in 2002:

The Boy That Made a Decision
Devon Finney, 4th Grade

> Once upon a time there was a boy named Mark. Mark was 13 years old. He lived on the corner of 9th and Master Street. Mark liked to play basketball at Cruz Playground. One day, some boys came over to Mark and asked him if he wanted to go with them to throw rocks at the windows in empty houses. Mark knew that breaking out windows was wrong, but he did not want to tell the boys no. He did not want them to be mad with him. So Mark made up an excuse so that he did not have to go.
>
> The next day the boys asked him to go with them again. Again, Mark made up an excuse. Marcel, the leader of the group, told Mark that he better come with them the next day. Mark decided not to come out of the house that day. Mark told his older brother that Marcel and the other boys had threatened him that he had better go with them to throw rocks at old windows. Mark's brother asked

him if he wanted him to go with him to the playground. Mark thought about what he should do all night.

The next day Mark decided to go to the playground alone. The kids were already there playing basketball. Mark had his basketball too. He began to play ball. Marcel and his boys came over and approached Mark. Marcel asked Mark if he was ready to throw some rocks. Mark looked Marcel right in the eyes and said, "NO!" Mark said, "I made my decision. I do not want to get in trouble. I'm going to play basketball."

Marcel got mad. Marcel and the boys made a circle around Mark. The other kids who were playing basketball saw what was happening. They ran and got John, who was the coach. John told Marcel and the other boys to go away and leave Mark alone. John told the boys that Mark had made his decision to stay at the playground and if they continued to threaten Mark, he would tell their parents and then call the police.

Marcel got scared. He decided to leave Mark alone. Marcel said, "We didn't want Mark to play anyway." Mark knew that Marcel just said that because he was scared that John would call the police. John looked at Mark and said, "Sometimes we all have to make a decision to do the right thing. I think you made the right decision and I am so proud of you"

Mark smiled.

A Slave Girl's Cry
Desiree Grant, 6th Grade

"Every day I wear this cocoa brown skin and holey rags for clothing on my back." Henrietta stared at herself in the cracked mirror nailed to the wall of her bedroom at Master Stevenson's plantation.

"Oh, Mama, I just hate living this way, having to prepare supper for people who aren't even of my kind, and who torture me every given moment of my life," said Esther, Henrietta's 13-year-old daughter, who had been under ownership of Master Stevenson since the day she was born.

Esther despises slavery and being under captivity because of all the cruel things she has seen done to her friends and relatives. She has been cut by sharp looks, and the mistreating of her foes has bruised her heart. Not only did she hate slavery, but she dreamt of escaping from Master's plantation, knowing that to pass the steel bars that stood seven feet outside of her window was impossible, for there was only an inch space and she had no tools to saw them down with.

Because Esther was enslaved since birth, she'd never experienced freedom, which caused her to be even more anxious. Many nights she would take fire escape plans and draw copies to use as an escape plan for freedom.

"Mama, why do those people treat us so wrongly? Is it not us who cook their food, wash their clothes and clean their dirty dishes? I think we should all flee this place," said Esther.

"I reckon that isn't possible," Henrietta refuted.

"Yes, all we have to do is cause a riot and stampede. We're guaranteed to knock that gate down with Big Gunther," Esther insisted.

"That imagination of yours is getting a little too adventurous," Henrietta confronted.

Inside, Henrietta believed that Esther's dream could come true, but from past experiences, Esther didn't need any encouragement. Esther would think of things that no one else ever thought of. Also, Esther's ways were very eerie, seeing that in the years she had been alive, she'd had more whippings than years she's been a slave girl.

Many rules were broken every day. In fact,

Henrietta and Esther were breaking the most important one of being on time. When rules were broken, whippings were given out. If the child broke a rule, the parent was given the penalty too, but if the parent broke a rule, they were given the penalty alone. In this case, it meant two whippings for Henrietta.

Later that evening when the slave owners gathered in their gowns and tuxedos, Henrietta hung from the pole, praying to God, saying, "Lord, I know that only you can work miracles and do miraculous things, but at this moment, I pray that you send an angel to take me out of this harm and danger."

And just as Esther arrived to the site, she saw her mother lying in a pool of blood, not exhaling.

"No, Mama, don't leave me all alone in this cruel world," Esther whispered to her mother's dead body.

The Lord had answered Henrietta's prayers but now Esther's were in the works.

Day after day Esther would stare at her mother's old rags thinking that no matter what the clothes looked like, they looked extravagant with her mother in them.

"Mama, during these hard times when I need you most, you aren't here, but during those days when I would run to you with open arms, I didn't deserve or appreciate your loving and kind spirit. If only I could turn back the hands of time. Oh, Mama, I miss you so dearly," Esther said. "I know everything happens and I shouldn't question God, but I wish He would have taken anyone but you—including me."

"No sleeping on the job!" Master Stevenson screamed, "Now, git!"

"I don't have to put up with your no good treating," Esther mumbled under her breath. "I'm gonna be like Mama is—FREE!" After Esther spoke those words she started thinking about the freedom escape plans she had made the night before.

Esther went back to her room to get her worn wicker basket, which held her escape plans drawn and labeled by herself. The only problem was that the particular plan she was looking for was mysteriously missing. Esther began to panic. She began to think that her mother's life was taken because of the missing plan.

Esther decided to show the escape plans to her best friend Adeline. "Do you know how much trouble you can get into if Master sees this?" Adeline asked.

"Yeah," Esther answered.

"Do you even care?" Adeline wondered aloud.

"No," Esther answered. "That's what's wrong with you. You're always worrying about what's gonna happen."

"Well, excuse me if I care about—" Adeline began.

Master Stevenson was standing behind her and she knew by that chill in her spine that she always got that he was around.

"If you weren't talking, maybe you would have something done. Now pull those corn crops," Master yelled. "Yes, sir," Adeline replied.

Master Stevenson walked away slowly with his black cloak swinging from side to side.

"Later, I am going to talk to Big Gunther about that sledge hammer he uses to build sheds for Master," Esther informed Adeline.

"Good luck," said Adeline.

"Who needs luck when they have God?" Esther responded while turning away.

When Esther reached Big Gunther's shed, she saw a wanted poster nailed to the sidewall. It read:

WANTED
Bertha Johnson
Runaway Slave
Reward: $10,000

In her mind, Esther was saying, "Master know he ain't givin' nobody that kind of money, he ain't even got two pennies."

While Esther was talking to Big Gunther, she was overheard by Master and punished greatly. Her punishment made her die the same death as her mother.

*   *   *

The culmination of Erwin's first year at Gesu was a novella written by the 7th graders. Through a grant from the Disney Creative Classroom Fund and Backe Communications, the students received tape recorders with which they could interview family members; each then wrote a short story. Following class discussion of the stories and ways to connect the characters and plots, the fifteen students unified their plot lines into a novella about saving a neighborhood church.

It may say a lot about the young authors' lives that many of the chapters relate tales of broken homes in various forms and contain more than a little violence, especially against children. But in the end Erwin could describe it as "an inspiring story about what people can accomplish when they come together and work for a common purpose."

Saving St. Peter's
(From the Introduction)

The "Yellow Yonder" was once the wealthiest section of Cyprus City. It was called the yellow yonder because life seemed to be forever sunny. . . . Only millionaires lived there, and their elevation above the rest of the people in the city was so important that the residents of Yellow Yonder had it isolated from the rest of the city. The people who lived there didn't do things for themselves. They had servants to do everything for them. . . .

Years later . . . A once wealthy community now lies in ruins. . . . Eventually, all of the kids in the neighborhood join together to try and get the church reopened. As a result of this mission to save the church, the kids realize that they are connected a little more than they think. . . .

(From the concluding chapter)
It was the day of the talent show, a fundraiser for saving the church, and all the families from Blue Yonder were there.

. . . Everyone got in place and Mr. Banks went on stage to start his speech. The church was filled. There was not an empty seat.

"Good afternoon, neighbors and friends of neighbors. We are all here for one reason, and it's all because of the children. The children cleaned the church and helped raise money with the help of Mr. Jack Lafayette and his daughter Christan. You see, these children had a dream. Do you know what that dream was? Well, if you don't, I'll tell you. Their dream was to bring the neighborhood back together. As you can see, their dream came true. We are all here together. We used to be rich in money. Now we are rich in love. And it is all because of our children. Our beautiful children. Give them a hand. Now first up we have Ricardo El Mondez and Marlow Banglback, also known as Black & Gold." . . .

After the talent show, they had a block party. It was the best party in the world. There were games, music, dancing, food, and, most importantly, there was laughter. Everyone was laughing and talking and eating together. . . . That day the neighborhood learned, "United we stand, divided we fall."

Erwin introduces her young writers to the variety of forms a cautious section at a time and works hard with them on punctuation and grammar. During my visits, 6th graders were tackling myths, 5th graders the short story, and 4th graders tall tales, one of the latter a particularly clever take on "The Strongest Man in the World."

My favorite moment occurred when Erwin told the children quietly that there was too much talking, which would slow down their work. One girl's plaintive response would resonate with any writer who has struggled with a passage: "My work is slowing down, and I'm not even talking."

Chapter VII

Children and Faith

"I don't think you ever can get too much about the word of God,"

Laura Ann Hood, fresh out of college, was excited after her first visit to the Gesu School. For Laura Ann, a teacher and superintendent of Sunday school at her church in Northeast Philadelphia, supervisor of a summer Bible school for seven years, teaching religion to little children is something important she wants to do with her life. That made Gesu a natural fit to her. "I had a good background in religion, had a lot of projects collected, and I wanted to carry on, to do some character development things which I knew I couldn't do in a public school district."

For Gesu religion at the kindergarten level introduces the children to a God who loves them individually, passionately, intensely. Or as Laura Ann puts it, "God loves you, God loves you no matter what, God made the world and he loves everything in it. He loves you just as much as he loves her and her and her.

"I try to incorporate religion in everything I do. We talk about emotions. I read them books: 'I know my mommy loves me, I know my daddy loves me.' They need to know that people are there. They need to know about praying. We thank God for food."

Gesu is a Catholic school, no question about that. But one of the awesome qualities about this little school is how it brings together people of different faiths—Lutheran like Hood, Presbyterian, Jewish, Catholic—in support of children of different faiths—some of them Catholic, some unchurched, a majority Baptist. Faith matters here; but education matters most of all.

Gesu's independence, which followed the suppression of the parish, means that it is not a part of the school system operated by the Archdiocese of Philadelphia, but it affiliates by choice in a number of important ways. It buys textbooks from the archdiocesan education office and receives Federally funded school lunches through the archdiocesan system. Sister Ellen attends regular meetings of Philadelphia Catholic school principals, just as principals of many other private academies in the city and suburbs do.

Gesu uses the official curriculum of the archdiocese although it does not have to. This curriculum worked before the school became independent and continues to work well, Sister Ellen said, so there is no reason to change. "It's very successful. The Catholic schools of Philadelphia are very successful."

The division of subjects in the curriculum looks much like that of a public school, with the obvious exception of religion:

For grades 1 and 2, 25 hours of class are scheduled per week. Of this, 15 hours are devoted to Integrated Language Arts (ILA), which consists of reading, writing, thinking, listening, speaking; just under 4 hours to mathematics; 45 minutes each to science, social studies, music, art, and 30 minutes to physical education. Religion is to occupy 2 hours of instruction time, or about one-tenth of the school calendar.

For grades 3 and 4, 27 hours-plus weekly: ILA instruction is scheduled for 12 hours, and math again nearly 4 hours; science and social studies are stepped up to 2 hours each per week, and music, art, computer education, and physical education each receive 45 minutes per week (usually a 45-minute session once a week). Religion increases to just under three hours weekly.

In grades 5-8, the academic week extends to 27.5 hours or 5.5 hours per day, excluding arrival, dismissal, recess, and lunch hours. ILA is reduced to 8 hours-plus per week; math is increased to 4 hours, and science and social studies to nearly 4 hours. Computer ed, physical ed, music, and art can vary between 45 and 55 minutes weekly. Religion is now just over 3 hours, or about one hour in every seven.

A critical connection at Gesu is to the I.H.M. community, whose nuns have been teaching at the school for more than a century. During one conversation with Sister Ellen, I mentioned my experience teaching college students who were woefully weak in grammar and punctuation. I said that an important part of my own instruction in grammar had come through diagramming sentences, but that students today didn't know how to diagram, except for a few who had gone to Catholic schools. "We do diagramming every day, beginning in 5th grade," Ellen answered immediately. "It's a daily diet." She explained:

"[In our] community, the Immaculate Heart Sisters, part of our educational baggage, the things we bring with us to school, are what we call 'maintenance sheets.' We invented the idea. The community publishes them, and you have them with you. It maintains skills. Every day there's a little review on the skills that you have studied. Every lesson begins that way.

"For example, every day the math lesson begins with the math maintenance sheet. There are five columns, five problems a day, not what the kids are doing that day [but review from earlier lessons]. If in 5th grade you're learning fractions, the columns might be long division or three-digit multiplication, things that you're going to forget because you're doing fractions now. The same is true for the integrated language arts, which is their reading, writing, spelling, grammar. Diagramming is in there."

The relationship between Gesu and the I.H.M. community is fundamental and historic. Founded in 1845 on the frontier of Monroe, Michigan (now an urban manufacturing town between Detroit and Toledo), I.H.M. currently numbers more than 600 sisters who live in seven states as well as Chile and Peru. More than half the sisters are teachers, trained for instruction from preschool to adult education, including Montessori and daycare programs. But changing times and changing ways of life have reduced their numbers sharply from the 1950s, and as the congregation ages, more of the sisters spend their time with literacy programs for adults, English instruction for immigrants, and hospital ministering.

I.H.M. sisters have taught at Gesu since 1891, when they joined the Sisters of Notre Dame who had come earlier to teach the girls in the parish school. But their dwindling roster has had its effect, leaving Sister Ellen and Sister Pat as the only members of the I.H.M. community currently serving at Gesu. A nun for more than four decades, Sister Pat came to Gesu as a 7th-grade teacher just after it became independent, one of five I.H.M. sisters at the time. As the holder of a counseling degree, she was soon asked by Father Bur and Sister Ellen to work with troubled children and their families, and in 1999 became the school's full-time counselor, a soothing voice for a child "acting out."

"Alcohol, drugs, divorce, there's no neighborhood in this country that's free of that," Sister Pat said, "but here the kids have to deal with it more, plus the violence they are exposed to. Our kids are very resilient; considering what they have to cope with, it's phenomenal.

She believes the school offers consistency that is often lacking in their families. "Some of the families are stable, but the majority [probably are not]. I don't think that's out of neglect, it's out of necessity—single-parent families, parents working so long, their neighborhood." What makes a difference, Sister Pat said, is that "we're a happy place, we're a safe place for them. I think that's evident when strangers come into the school. They can get the temper of the place, and that's not false because children don't lie. You can't make a child perform [dishonestly]. There's no hiding the dirty laundry."

In a 2001 celebration of the I.H.M. ministry at Gesu, Father Bur observed that current conditions were in many ways similar to what the sisters faced when they arrived in 1891 to educate "Irish and other neighborhood boys, some of them hard scrabble kids.

". . . So begins a love affair between the sisters and the neighborhood families. This love affair continued through the new century, through the wars, through the Depression, through the departure of the Notre Dame sisters and the added responsibility of educating the girls, through the demographic changes that transformed the neighborhood from one of white immigrants to one of black immigrants from the South, through the civil disturbances of the '60s, through its abandonment by both white and black middle classes, to the neighborhood of today, struggling but still filled as always with families who have high aspirations for their children."

The sisters performed tasks that could have been, in Father Bur's estimation, beyond the Jesuits. "We Jesuits, sure enough, stuck with the school, too, through all these years. But none of us had the skills in teaching at the elementary level, none of us had the experience with children and their teachers, none of us could set the tone for the culture and traditions of the school, none of us had the patience . . . to stick with a troubled youngster until he or she made that transition to self-respect."

The I.H.M. community joined with the Society of Jesus to lobby for the continuation of the Gesu School after the parish suppression. "If closing the parish is like saying farewell to the Lord," said Father Bur, "keeping the school open is like continuing His work even in His absence. Keeping the school open is keeping alive the instructions about how to love, how to gain wisdom and how to live at peace."

"I suspect that in the absence of the sisters the school would have died either when the parish closed or even before," Father Bur said. Their presence, moreover, not only saved the school but also buttressed the neighborhood. "The sisters continue to create an oasis for children. They always brought into the school the best neighborhood traditions and values and melded them into the life of the school.

"They worked with the immigrant families that brought the traditions of outdoor processions to our neighborhood. They worked with the block clubs to counteract the attractions that our children felt to the neighborhood gangs that existed in both the culture of white youth and black youth. If the neighborhood is no longer so Catholic in population, the sisters brought into the school from the neighborhood the local traditions of religious art and music."

Father Bur praised the sisters' ability to carry out their community's mission statement in this new era. They continue "to challenge attitudes, lifestyles, and values which are in conflict with the word of God." They continue "to promote the human dignity of each person, especially the most abandoned." They continue "to acculturate themselves into the rich diversity of the peoples with whom they share ministry in humility, friendship, and love." And they continue "to invite all they meet into the full sacramental life of the Church."

Religion, then, is an important part of the Gesu curriculum for reasons beyond the fact that this is a Catholic school. Instruction in religion, and especially the values that accompany it, is important because the parents desire it that way. "People appreciate it, they want it, that's the reason they send their children here," said Sister Ellen. "They want the values, they want the morals, they want the kids to have a sense of religion, a sense of God."

As many as half the children come from families with no church membership. Of the other half, by far the most are Baptist; about one in six is Catholic although not necessarily active in the church. Children notice the differences between Catholic instruction and what they are accustomed to—"In my church the whole body goes down in the pit to be baptized; in the Catholic church they just pour water over your head"—so teachers encourage them to ask questions, discuss the differences, make comparisons.

Through the school's standard Catholic textbooks, the children must memorize the Ten Commandments and the seven sacraments and say all the Catholic prayers and the rosary, no matter their religion. Since religion is an academic subject, the children are tested and graded on how well they do.

On the theory that it is never too soon to begin religious instruction, at Gesu it starts with kindergarten classes like Laura Ann Hood's and even pre-kindergarten. Everyone goes to regular masses, sometimes celebrated in the school library or gymnasium. "We're a warm weather church," Sister Ellen said with a chuckle. "They don't heat the [Gesu] church, so we go there in September, October, November; December is iffy, and we see how it works in winter and spring."

An 8th grade textbook, *Morality: A Course on Catholic Living*, includes chapters called "Sin and Forgiveness," "Finding the Sacred," and "Choosing Life," and specific short explanations about "Catholic Teachings," such as the effects of original sin, the mass, pornography, and the seal of confession. For example, the explanation, "About Scandal," reads: "The Church teaches that 'scandal is an attitude or behavior which leads another to do evil' (Catechism, 2284). Friends have tremendous influence over one another. When we use our power and influence to persuade others to do wrong, instead of urging them to do what is right, we are guilty of the sin of scandal. We show ourselves to be an enemy rather than a friend."

Gesu also offers, as part of its religion courses, a block of instruction in human sexuality, "which I think a lot of parents appreciate," said Sister Ellen. As early as 5th grade, a textbook called *Fully Alive* devotes sections to the stages of life: the family; male and female sexuality; responsibility, and living in a community.

The section called, "Created Sexual: Male and Female" begins with a verse from chapter 1 of Genesis, "God created man in his image . . . male and female he created them." Its sub-sections are titled, "We Are Wonderfully Made," which concerns individual and group relationships; "The Body System That Gives Life," with drawings of the body; "Human Fertility," containing explicit drawings of the adult male and female reproductive systems; and "Puberty," discussing the changes in one's body during that physically and emotionally difficult period.

The work "teaches [the children] the facts of life," said Sister Ellen, "but it also teaches them values, teaches them about chastity." She said that she has not had a single complaint about the sexuality program, or for that matter about any element of the school's religious instruction.

Cecilia Ross-Kent sees no conflict. A loyal Gesu parent, Ross-Kent and her husband are devoted members of the Mt. Sinai Tabernacle Baptist Church in North Philadelphia, she a deaconess and he a deacon who is studying to be a Baptist minister. "I don't think you ever can get too much about the word of God," Ross-Kent said. She realizes that Gesu teaches more about saints than her children are accustomed to at the Baptist church, which her son and two of her grandchildren attend with her and where they sing in the choir. But, "I haven't found anything that would contradict what they are taught in church. I don't feel that it's going to hurt them."

Maleeca Bryant, a practicing Baptist, is now a college student after graduating from Gesu and a strict Philadelphia Catholic high school; to her, there was "a big difference" in how those two taught religion. Gesu "makes you comfortable," she said, letting you "know things" but not demanding that you practice them. At her high school, "I learned what I was required to learn, and practiced only what I had to practice."

It is the combination of religious instruction and social values that makes the Gesu program work, said John DiIulio, Gesu trustee, University of Pennsylvania political scientist, and lifelong Catholic, who emphasizes the importance of teaching values in a Catholic school with a largely non-Catholic student population. "I think the Catholics have a bit of an advantage with respect to religion entering the public square, because part of Catholic social teaching is that faith without works is death," DiIulio said. "As Catholics, we have a long tradition, a couple of thousand years, and in this country since its inception, of doing missionary-type work with many people, and not being particularly hung up on whether they know their Hail Marys or not. . . .

"For Catholics in general, and Gesu in particular, having non-Catholic children there, Baptists, Muslims, whatever, there's a certain minimum that we insist on. We're a Catholic institution, so you're going to know you're in a Catholic institution. And you're going to hear about Jesus Christ, no doubt about it, and you're also going to hear about Jesus Christ from a Catholic perspective. We're not teaching reformation theology here. But then again we're not teaching Catholic theology. . . .

"This is 400-some kids who are experiencing a manifestation of Catholic social teaching. It's the best of Catholic social teaching: 'They're our kids. They're not the government's kids. They're not a corporation's kids.' That's different from a lot of faith-based approaches, and it's certainly different from the secular, professional, government breakdown.

"So Catholics have an advantage. It gets a little hairier when you're in an evangelical Christian mode, where in some sense you can't easily separate out the proselytizing and the religious sectarian worship from the delivery of service. We're able to compartmentalize a lot better. Or a lot worse [to some Catholics], depending on how you look at it. That's one of the reasons why we have Jewish board members. . . .

The Jewish board members quite agree, said Leonard Klehr, a lawyer and leader both in the Philadelphia civic community and its Jewish community, who sees no religious impediment to his support of Gesu. "The fact that there's a commitment to Christian values, and the Bible is taught, or other kinds of religious indoctrination if there is such, is of no moment to me. There are so many other valuable things being taught at the school—the most important of which is that learning is good and education is good. . . . To me, having kids in that kind of environment overrides any issues or factors of parochial schools.

"My view," said Klehr, "is that the leadership of both the Jesuits and the Immaculate Heart of Mary sisters is the under-pinning of the mission of the Gesu School, and that to them, all of the kids are children of God and are loved because they came of God. I see no issue with that on any religious grounds. The fact that people are on that mission gives the school its drive and enthusiasm and makes it the place it is."

So, yes, it's religion, but only partly, and social values, but only partly, and community needs, but only partly. It's mostly about the children, the children of God.

Chapter VIII

To Do What's Necessary

"You'd be amazed at how good the kids are at it. They're very perceptive of people's feelings."

A lthough Gesu's fundamental curriculum is, almost needless to say, much like that in other schools, even the apparently routine is a little different here. The school takes care to meet the special characteristics of its African-American student body and its working-class parent body. And overcoming inherent problems, it struggles to provide the extra-curricular activities like athletics that other schools offer.

Gesu seeks every opportunity to focus on black history and culture, notably during Black History Month in February. When I visited one of Eilise Moran's 8th grade classes, eight boys and nine girls, the children were exploring the Harlem Renaissance of the 1920s and '30s, not by rote but through presentations prepared individually or in teams. Moran first led an examination of Studs Terkel's oral-history style; next the class discussed the Great Depression, including a debate about the presidencies of Herbert Hoover and Franklin D. Roosevelt, before moving to the meaning of the Harlem Renaissance.

When the children took over, Moran critiqued not only their writing and oral presentations but also the audience skills of their listeners. One performance traced the pleasure and pain in the life of Billie Holliday. In another playlet, a *Time* magazine reporter interviewed Bill Robinson, including pointed questions about how "Bojangles" could allow himself to be racially stereotyped.

Political scientist John DiIulio calls projects like this part of Gesu's "smartly Afro-centric curriculum." It is a sensitive area. "That stuff can get very goofy very quickly," DiIulio said, "unless it's done with a real sense of the real children, from real families with real backgrounds, who happen to be African-American. It makes sense to hook into their culture, to hook into things that are coming to be important in their lives as African-American children. [But not to] go overboard; that can be patronizing."

*   *   *

Given more funds, and more confidence about how the children perform, Gesu has enriched its academic program. It has managed to step up arts offerings, recently adding a full-time art teacher. It appointed a full-time physical-education teacher for both boys and girls. It now has a full-time librarian.

The first "honors" course established for advanced students—mathematics, actually an introduction to algebra—was taught by Father Bur. Desmond Shannon, now a student at St, Joseph's Prep, found his freshman math course at this elite high school covered "the same things" as he had learned in the 8th grade at Gesu. Although math honors is the only instance of "tracking" by ability except for the specialized writing program, it could be used more, suggested Ronald Warren, also now at the Prep. Warren, who won seventeen different academic prizes when he graduated in 2001 (so did his classmate Kyle Carney), confessed that "In some classes things seemed repetitive." What does he do to keep from being bored? "I doodle a lot."

The school also has a full-time computer teacher. Children receive formal computer instruction from kindergarten through 8th grade. They are taught to type if necessary, with special help for the younger children on their letters. The 7th and 8th grade classrooms each have two computers, and all have at least one, new equipment seeming to arrive every day. The entire building is wired, every classroom Internet ready.

In extending its reach, the faculty is usually supplemented by volunteers under a program called ResponseAbility, something like the AmeriCorps, which is administered by Rosemont College in the western Philadelphia suburbs. Rosemont recruits graduates from colleges around the country for two years' service to inner-city education. The young men and women live together as a community (it is not a religious order), receiving room and board and a modest stipend; they can socialize and enjoy Philadelphia in addition to their commitment to its inner-city.

Gesu will take two volunteers a year (unless there is no faculty turnover), paying Rosemont a service fee much smaller than a teacher's salary. "We've had some really talented people," said Sister Ellen, and a number of them have remained as Gesu teachers after their volunteer period ended.

*   *   *

In a city where the Phillies, the Eagles, the Flyers, and the 76ers arouse bellowing emotion—pro and con—children want to talk about the games and to play them. How could Gesu not encourage sports? No one at the school has noticed any future Philly high-school basketball players like Wilt Chamberlain, but thanks to yeoman volunteer effort and timely contributions, both boys and girls are introduced to physical education and interscholastic competition. They are even an occasional force in Catholic Youth Organization leagues.

Gesu usually begins organized team play in the 6th grade, although track competition may begin in the 4th and girls can try out for cheerleader in the 5th. The school sponsors basketball teams and track and field for both boys and girls, baseball for boys, and softball and cheerleading for girls. It considered football, and eighty boys signed up, but 6th-grade teacher Phil Campbell, who became something of a one-person coaching staff soon after his arrival in 1997, was the only faculty member able to instruct them, so the idea was abandoned.

The school has had other sports setbacks, as in 2000 when the baseball team was suspended by the CYO. Although the team numbered seventeen players, when only seven showed up for three weekend games, the league dropped Gesu.

The attendance problem is related to the children's family environments. Some of them spend weekends in New Jersey or distant parts of Greater Philadelphia visiting grandparents or a parent they don't live with. Even closer, a parent who doesn't see his or her child regularly may not want to share precious visiting time with other people at a playing field. Parents also may work weekends or have transportation difficulties.

Since the school has no specific budget for sports equipment, the children help themselves with bake and candy sales or selling magazine subscriptions. The basketball teams were outfitted handsomely by the Philadelphia sporting-goods company called And 1—sets of twenty-five jerseys, shorts, socks, and sneakers for boys and girls. (The next year, the girls brought back their complete uniforms; Campbell had to replace the boys' sneakers.) For baseball, the coach bought balls and bats at a discount store and found fifteen blue-and-white pinstripe shirts, on which were sewn "Gesu" and numbers.

For all the difficulties, Gesu athletes have managed surprising successes. The 2000-01 girls basketball team, with only seven players, won 33 games and lost 3 in their league; then in the regional playoffs they ran into a tall, fast, disciplined team from Bucks County and discovered they were out of their league. The girls track team has produced city medalists at 100 and 200 meters, along with a 4 X 100 meter relay team good enough to compete in the Penn Relays. The 2000-01 boys basketball team compiled 28 victories against 4 losses to win the regional championship. Several graduates have gone on to varsity basketball in high school, and a couple have played at the college level.

Mostly, though, it's not the won-and-lost records but the fun. Campbell recalled with glee his first Gesu baseball team. Since many of the boys had never played before, he had to teach them the absolute fundamentals, throwing and catching a ball, "until they got the hang of it." They were so excited at their first game that "you'd have thought we were playing at Veterans Stadium." After its opponent took a 3-0 lead, Gesu scored a run, and "you'd have thought we won the World Series." Then another run. Wow! 3-2. After that, Campbell noted, the game fell apart, "but you couldn't take those two runs away from them."

*   *   *

Although the school's usual practice is not to track children by academic ability except for writing and more recently math, it does offer specialized help for those diagnosed with learning disabilities. For many years Gesu lacked the capability to deal with these children—"We didn't have a lot of choices," Sister Ellen said—so that it was forced to arrange transfers for many of them. Yet the school doesn't like to give up on anybody, and in some cases parents lobbied successfully to have their children remain in Gesu because they considered the atmosphere so comforting. Finally, in 1999, after looking disapprovingly at a number of special-education programs in Philadelphia schools, the Gesu faculty developed its own program for learning-disabled children.

In an effort to avoid stigma, Gesu calls this a "resource room" instead of "special education." Sister Ellen notices that as children reach adolescence, 7th and 8th graders, they are more likely to resist the unusual attention, but that "if the experience is pleasant they don't feel stigmatized. A lot depends on the teacher," and the special-ed teachers try hard to create rapport with—to be popular with—their charges

Gesu teachers try to spot children with learning disabilities quickly, sometimes as early as kindergarten. If, for example, a 2nd grader is not reading at grade level, a professional counselor will be called in to test the child's IQ, vision, and hearing. If a problem is confirmed, the child's parents will be called to a meeting with the counselor and teachers, who will describe the difficulty and recommend solutions.

A former teacher recalled one little girl who appeared at school irregularly and often in a zombie-like state. It was soon discovered that she had been raped by her mother's parolee boy friend. A quick solution, more likely in a large school setting, might have been to diagnose her with Attention Deficit Disorder and place her in a special education program until she dropped out. But Gesu's faculty insisted on treating the girl "as a whole person," taking up one problem after another, using education, religion, and common sense, until they had helped her put herself together. Today the girl has earned a place in a good boarding school.

A full-time teacher and full-time teacher's aide work in the resource room with small groups, no more than four at a time, and often individually. They usually focus on the Integrated Language Arts (ILA), using a story or chapter of a novel as a framework for grammar, writing, spelling. If a child cannot learn that way, teachers will turn to the basic phonetic approach, the drills of bat-cat-sat. With one method or another, and sometimes both, children given this special attention tend to catch up on their reading levels.

*   *   *

Visitors to the Gesu School invariably comment on the openness and cheerful demeanor of the children. Friendly and well-behaved. Most of the time. But what do you do when children prove troublesome? Especially, since many of these children come from homes where anger is commonplace and expressed openly, or the mean streets teach ugly lessons of violence?

A child might challenge the authority of a teacher—as children occasionally will, or a group of children might pick on one of their classmates—as they will, or start arguing with each other—as some inevitably will. At Gesu discipline is important, and enforced. And the children and their families know this from the start. As with every element of the children's lives at school, their families must be active participants.

One way to avoid unsettling competition is the dress code. The children all wear uniforms, identical from kindergarten to 8th grade. The boys wear blue trousers and a white, collared Gesu polo shirt. The girls begin in blue-and-gray plaid culottes and white Gesu blouses, graduating to skirts in 6th grade so they feel more grown up. Parents pay for the uniforms, to the extent they can afford it, and the school annually holds an exchange for children who have outgrown their uniforms, the way fancy prep schools hold ice-skate exchanges.

Gesu's rules are stated clearly in the parent-student handbook distributed to every family, titled, "It Takes a Whole Village to Raise a Child." In a category called "Behavioral Standards and Expectations" are listed the rights and responsibilities of every student.

GESU SCHOOL STUDENT BILL OF RIGHTS

1. I have the right to learn without interference.

2. I have the right to work and play in a safe environment.

3. I have the right to move without interference.

4. I have the right to be touched by another person only when I choose.

5. I have the right to have my work respected.

6. I have the right to be listened to when I am speaking.

7. I have the right to get help when it is my turn.

8. I have the right to express my feelings appropriately and to have my feelings respected.

GESU SCHOOL STUDENT BILL OF RESPONSIBILITIES

1. I have the responsibility to allow others to learn. I have the responsibility to work at learning, stay on task and exercise effort.

2. I have the responsibility to do my homework daily.

3. I have the responsibility to care for myself and the environment so as not to endanger others.

4. I have the responsibility to manage my own body so that I do not touch others when they do not want to be touched.

5. I have the responsibility to respect the property of others.

6. I have the responsibility to keep my possessions where they belong.

7. I have the responsibility to respect the work of others.

8. I have the responsibility to take care of my work area.

9. I have the responsibility to listen and respond to others clearly, honestly and respectfully.

10. I have the responsibility to wait my turn and respect others' turn. I have the responsibility to ask for help when I need it.

11. I have the responsibility to express my feelings and opinions appropriately.

12. I have the responsibility to respect the feelings and opinions of others.

The handbook spells out student behavior that is "inappropriate and will require corrective action": "Disruptive behavior; disrespect for the rights of others; disrespect for an adult, e.g., answering back, having the last word; disrespect for school property; talking and/or running during a fire drill; running in the school building; throwing things in the classrooms, hallways, cafeteria, etc.; profane, obscene and vulgar language; fighting, verbally or physically, in school or school uniform; chewing gum or candy in classroom; violating dress code; failure to report to assigned class or to the office when sent out."

Behavior problems can lead to various "corrective measures," ranging from a personal session with a teacher to extra assignments, detention, and loss of privileges such as field trips or recess. A delinquent child is likely first to face Father Neil or Sister Pat, herself a former teacher who will counsel the children and their families; parents are always part of the process. There may be several conferences and several levels of remedies.

A nastier infraction—stealing, vandalism, fighting—can lead to immediate suspension from school. "There's zero tolerance for fighting," Sister Ellen said. And a student can be suspended or even expelled for possession of drugs, alcohol, or weapons, for leaving school during the day, or for physical abuse of a faculty or staff member. Authorities take a measured approach, tailoring the punishment to the student or the offense, and expulsion is a very last resort. If they decide that a child must leave Gesu, they work with the parents to arrange a transfer, perhaps to a nearby Catholic school; no child is shunted off to the street.

The harsh but rare remedy of expulsion troubles Sister Ellen, and she still shudders at what she calls "a mistake I made, a big mistake," several years ago. She said that she had not expected to tell me the story at all, then changed her mind because it illustrated real life at the school.

The first year that Gesu had a four-year-old program one boy was a particular behavior problem. He was dismissed from class almost every day, sent to the secretary's office, where he would lie back on a chair and sleep, sometimes for hours. Teachers were aware of him all the time: he couldn't listen, couldn't walk in line, couldn't or wouldn't follow instructions to his group. When he brought a huge hunting knife to school one day, Ellen called the four-year-old's mother. You have to take him home, the principal said. He is too immature, not ready for school, a disruption to everyone. You can try again next year.

No longer in school, left alone at home, one afternoon he was playing with matches in his second-floor apartment and set the house on fire. He was the only person in the house that firemen could not bring out safely.

Does Ellen blame herself? "No, I don't blame myself, but I feel bad that we didn't do something else, that I didn't find an alternative way to deal with his behavior. Yes, I thought that if he were in school at 2 that afternoon, he wouldn't have done that. Trust me, that's the last four-year-old I ever put out like that."

*   *   *

Obviously the Gesu authorities counsel and discipline as necessary; it is part of their responsibility. At another level, however, the optimum way to resolve disputes among the children—optimum in the sense that they themselves learn how to cope with their problems—is called the Peer Mediation program. It is directed by the 8th-grade teacher, Eilise Moran, who earned her master's degree at Lesley College in Cambridge, Massachusetts, with a concentration in conflict resolution.

Peer mediation begins with an eight-week training period, open to 5th through 8th graders, girls and boys, anyone who wants to participate—even if they are known to have problems themselves. "From the get-go, we don't tell anybody not to join, even if I know this kid has bigger problems him or herself," Moran said. "I don't shut them down. If a child is in conflict all the time, and wants to be a peer mediator, it shows they want the skills, they know there are problems."

As usual at Gesu, with little spare time or spare room, organizing the training is not easy. Moran must collect the children during lunch period once or twice a week and take them to a room where they eat lunch, then work on their mediation lesson. Yet even the lunch hour can be overscheduled. "There are so many things," Moran said, "and it's hard to get them. They need free time."

Moran begins by helping the children understand the nature of conflict, its causes, the emotions that enter into it, how conflict escalates. They talk about anger and its degrees from annoyance to outrage. They learn how to become astute listeners—"active listening"—able to hear someone tell a story and paraphrase what they have heard. "You'd be amazed at how good the kids are at it," said Moran. "They're very perceptive of people's feelings. They're good at noticing things like body gestures, picking up on all kinds of stuff."

Subjects of the mediation are remarkably cooperative; their very presence together demonstrates that they both want to solve their problems. "Once they come," Moran said, "they're so in awe of the process, it's nice to see. They see that here are two peers of mine who are actually going to be able to talk with me, work with me, and work this out, as opposed to a disciplinarian, the principal or a teacher, being authoritarian and telling me what to do."

The trained student mediators work in pairs with their squabbling peers, one listening and paraphrasing, the other monitoring. Moran is in the room as well, since the children are not to be left alone, but she tries to avoid participating as much as possible.

Often the problems between children are ongoing, have existed for years, but the peer mediators refuse to "dig up the past," and rather deal with the problem at hand. Their toughest single problem is rumors, because rumors usually involve a whole class, a group tormenting one child. Something dangerous, such as actual fighting, is not for peer mediators; that is dealt with firmly by school authorities.

Since Moran teaches five classes in the morning and one in the afternoon every day, I asked if she received a salary bonus for her peer mediation work, She smiled at the question, answered no, and said that every teacher was expected to do something extra at the school.

Her enthusiasm and willingness to work reminded me of something Sister Ellen had said during our discussion about the dwindling number of I.H.M. sisters—that Eilise was the kind of young woman who, in a different era, might have become a nun. So I asked Eilise what she thought about that. "Absolutely, she's right, it's totally true," Moran said. "My mother went into the convent [and left, then married], and I'm very much like my mother. My parents [her father is a lawyer] are both pretty religious people. I'm sure I would have followed the same path my mother did, and probably for the same reasons she did. I probably would have left as well; I don't know."

Given Sister Ellen's anxiety about the future of her I.H.M. order, I asked Moran, "Why is it that women like you don't become nuns?" She paused. "The other forces of culture in society are so much stronger—that's just what it boils down to. You might have to come from a background that people had religious in their families. That pushes you. My parents were open to anything. But I remember having conversations about this with my mother while I was in high school, and it just made sense to follow another path."

Eilise was the second of five girls in her family, all of whom attended Catholic schools through college—four of them products of Jesuit universities, one who slipped away to Notre Dame. After graduating from Boston College, Eilise volunteered through the ResponsAbility program to work for two years on the Lower East Side of Manhattan, living with nine others in a large-roomed former convent, beginning graduate work while interning at a small Catholic school. She had always known she wanted to teach and "from that experience I knew I wanted to teach in the inner-city."

She went straight from that internship to Gesu, attracted not least by the Jesuit character of the school. "My education, and certainly the Jesuits had a lot to do with this, [encouraged] women: do you want your voice to be heard? Not that sisters don't have that ability, but they're definitely assuming a role that doesn't have that voice, as far as the church is concerned. I hope I have a voice here at Gesu." It seems clear that she does.

*　　　*　　　*

Having provided classes from kindergarten through 8th grade for many years, Gesu began in 1995 a small pre-kindergarten program for four-year-olds. As soon as space can be arranged, the school plans to institute full pre-kindergarten classes for both three and four-year-olds; it is Sister Ellen's highest academic priority. And she sees an additional benefit: Increased programming at all levels lifts some of the burden from the children's harried parents. "Our parents are really good, dedicated to their kids," Ellen said, "but unfortunately most of them are single parents who have a job. I watch them come in after school, 6 at night, a mother gets off the subway, walks up here, picks up two kids, goes back to the subway.

"It's a haaaaarrrd [she stretches the word] life. She takes her two kids home on the subway, she's got to bathe them, got to feed them, got to do homework. She's got to get them clean clothes for tomorrow. I don't know if she feels like reading a story while she's tucking them in. I think for a lot of our parents, that's how their life goes. And it starts that way almost as soon as the kids are born. That's why quality daycare, early daycare, is so important."

A version of daycare, buttressed by disciplined education, is part of Gesu's service to its community. Children start arriving about 7 in the morning, usually brought by mothers who must head off to work. Classes begin officially at 8, although teachers may start them a bit earlier, and officially end at 2:45 p.m.

Then Gesu shifts to an ambitious after-school schedule. About 80 to 90 children remain, most of them among the youngest in school, but the program is designed to be more than a baby-sitting service. Under a supervisory teacher, assisted by four adult volunteers and student volunteers from St. Joseph's University, the children do their homework first, then educational projects, and occasionally take trips.

Twice a week a group goes to Rosemont School of the Holy Child for concentrated computer training, and once a week some take lessons at the Arthur Ashe Youth Tennis Center. An organization called Black Women in Sports provides fencing lessons, complete with outfits, masks, foils. A theater club prepares assorted entertainments, plays, a Christmas show, a Halloween parody. "The place is pretty busy," a teacher said mildly.

Then there's the "Homework Club" for students who appear to have trouble doing homework on their own, either because they lack self-discipline or because of problematic circumstances at home. Teachers can assign students to Homework Club, which they are not allowed to leave until the work is finished—"mandatory sentencing" someone called it.

Some children don't leave school until 6 in the evening, which is about the time Sister Ellen leaves. She will have been there since 6:30 that morning.

Chapter IX

Lessons of the Past

"The change at Gesu was dramatic. There would be no more parish. . . "

This is a story of how the Gesu School has flourished in its first decade of independence, but to appreciate fully that story one must understand something about the city of Philadelphia, and its environs, its citizens of the 18th century, and the 19th, and the 20th, what they gave and what they took, how they and their city grew and changed

Philadelphia was the first city of the United States before there was a United States. "A true eighteenth-century metropolis," David McCullough called it in his monumental biography *John Adams*, "the largest, wealthiest city in British America, and the most beautiful. Visitors wrote in praise of its 'very exactly straight streets,' its 'many fair houses and public edifices,' and of the 'broad, tidal Delaware' . . . "

Laid out in a neat grid by the Quaker William Penn in 1682 as a "greene countrie towne," Philadelphia had grown, by the time of the American Revolution, to a population of more than 24,000, larger than New York and nearly twice the size of Boston. "Swarms of people moved up and down the sidewalks and spilled into the streets," according to McCullough. "At no point in the American continent could so many human beings be seen in such close proximity or in such variety. . . ." Yet from the start Philadelphia was also roomier than Boston, with its crooked streets, and New York, with its congestion and squalor; lower land prices would allow immigrants more elbow room than they would ever have dreamed of in the old country.

Its beckoning port and thriving commerce quickly attracted ambitious entrepreneurs and yeomen alike, who embarked on tiny sailing vessels, mostly from the British Isles and neighboring northern Europe. Not surprisingly, congregations of Irish Quakers, victims of poor crops and English religious prejudices, were among the earliest to follow William Penn to his City of Brotherly Love, and the city also attracted sizable numbers of a determined breed known as the "Scotch-Irish." Mainly

Presbyterian and thus unhappily treated under the Church of England, they had been lured from Scotland to the land and purported religious freedom of Northern Ireland. Disappointed again, many soon opted for the promise of the New World and were among the first citizens of Philadelphia to declare for the rebels against King George III.

Philadelphia built ships to sail from its own port and by the mid-19th Century it was building locomotives for its railroads—eight different lines in the city before the Civil War with eight different terminals. It spawned dozens of factories as the Industrial Revolution arrived, some employing the astonishing total of 100 or more workers. It clothed Americans from their caps to their socks, the leading textile city of the nation.

As the Civil War began, Philadelphia had grown to 50,000 people, nearly one-third foreign born. Ironically, as sociologists of the period observe, the City of Brotherly Love treated everyone well except abolitionists and free blacks, who, no matter their proven talents in the skilled trades, were shunted aside for each succeeding wave of immigrants.

After the war, and especially in the late 19th century and early 20th century, immigrants were arriving in the United States by the millions from all over Europe. A majority shared the Catholic religion, yet held firm to their national identities. In his study *American Catholic*, Charles Morris wrote, "Italian priests refused to baptize Lithuanians, Poles detested Czechs, Germans contended with Irish." The result was ethnic parishes, sometimes almost adjoining one another; in the years 1900 to 1930, "Italian" parishes opened in Philadelphia at the rate of one a year.

The Irish arrived earlier than most. A few Irish had lived in Philadelphia since colonial days, but the great migration began, of course, at the time of the potato famine in 1846-47 (by 1850 Dublin was the only city with more Irish than London or New York, and Philadelphia was the sixth-ranking Irish city in the

101

world). They were to be the largest foreign-born group in Philadelphia for the remainder of the century.

The Irish were like most other immigrant groups in important respects: poor, largely unlettered, willing to work at almost any job in their desperate effort to earn a place in this strange but promising new land. Yet unlike many others, Italians, for example, who had arrived from tumultuous towns and cities, the Irish were children of the land.

As the urban historians John Modell and Lynn H. Lees noted, the population of Ireland had expanded rapidly near the end of the 18th Century and early in the 19th. Even laborers could afford to marry early and more or less control their own destiny on leased land, and they could subdivide the land as their children grew to start families of their own; smaller parcels could support a family when potatoes replaced grain as the principal crop. Eventually, though, subdivision resulted in farms too small to raise a family; more men found themselves reduced to day laborers, and family life changed; marriages came later and later, or not at all.

An alternative was to seek opportunities in the city, for the young women as well as the men. At first this usually meant Dublin and Belfast, because Ireland had few places that qualified as urban centers, essentially no urban structure to absorb landless immigrants. Increasing numbers crossed the narrow sea to Liverpool and Manchester; some of the more adventurous tried London, and soon the United States, as a critical mass began to build; and with the famine, Irish were streaming across the Atlantic.

But cities like Boston, New York, and Philadelphia were foreign to them in more ways than geography. ". . . the Irish in their homeland have been and are, even today, singularly rural, and their transition from the Irish countryside to the vast complexity of American cities represents a journey from one edge of the continuum of social organization to the other," wrote the social historian Dennis J. Clark in his book *The Irish in Philadelphia*. In an essay for *The Peoples of Philadelphia: A history of ethnic groups and lower-class life, 1790-1940*, Clark, a native Philadelphian, wrote:

> . . . the Irish experienced all the misfortunes of slum conditions as an introduction to urban living. As undesirable newcomers, they were consigned by economics and custom to the least desirable areas at the edge of the city proper . . . the city's first pattern of ethnic ghetto living. In the worst streets of these districts, overcrowding, dilapidation, and disease extracted a grim toll.

Laying the rails, tending the threading machines, the Irish began to work their way out of the slums. Yet even as they grew in important number, and sank roots into their new home, the Irish did not amass the civic power in Philadelphia that their compatriots did in Boston and New York. The Philadelphia Protestant establishment was too well entrenched and a comfortably Republican machine would not easily surrender political control.

Still, the Irish did have significant advantages over other immigrant classes. For one, they spoke, if not quite the Queen's English, at least a language that would allow them to participate in mainstream life. What they had going for them most of all, though, was the church. Closely tied to the Catholic church in Ireland as nearly all of them were, they arrived in the new land to find the international church structure in place. Besides providing the religious underpinning they knew so well, this meant a center to gather, a chance to meet fellow souls, and social services for those in need. It meant, critically, a school system that could prepare children to advance further than their elders in the American workplace and society.

The church's plan, according to historian Morris, "was to make it possible for an American Catholic to carry out almost every activity of life—education, health care, marriage and social life, union membership, retirement and old-age care—in a distinctly Catholic environment."

What became the Gesu parish eventually did all that and more, but it was created for one specific reason: education. Not surprising since this was a Jesuit undertaking and the Society of Jesus has been for centuries respected for its educational leadership. In his book *Jesuit Saturdays*, Father William J. Byron, himself a graduate of St. Joseph's Prep in Philadelphia and a former president of the Catholic University of America, said, "Values from another century, the 16th century of Ignatius of Loyola, are indeed alive and well in an impressive range of Jesuit secondary and middle schools that offer macro-hopes along with school-based solutions to this century's problems. No wonder Jesuits and their lay colleagues want to spend their working lives here."

In the United States such Jesuit colleges and universities as Georgetown, Fordham, Loyola of Maryland, Boston College, and Loyola of Chicago, and such Jesuit secondary schools as St. Joseph's Prep and Gonzaga in Washington, D.C., are among the nation's most highly regarded educational institutions.

The Jesuits established St. Joseph's College in Philadelphia in 1851 on the site of St. Joseph's Chapel, the first Catholic church in the city, Willing's Alley near the corner of Fourth and Walnut Streets; one of its neighbors was the old state house that is now known as Independence Hall.

The site was roomy enough in its early days, but as with many urban colleges right up to the present, the city caught up with the neighborhood, and when the Jesuits decided that St. Joseph's needed more room, they bought a chunk of land out in open country. They paid $45,000 for a square bounded by 17th and 18th streets, and Stiles and Thompson, about three miles from

Willing's Alley, and two years later dispatched an ambitious priest, the Rev. Burchard Villiger, to build it up.

Villiger, who was then 49 years old, was a native Swiss who had grown up in the face of anti-Catholic bias and had barely entered the Jesuit order when the Society was banished from Switzerland. Ordained in the United States at the age of 31, he began his career at St. Joseph's College the year it opened, then moved quickly through a series of responsible positions—provincial (chief administrator) of the Jesuits' Maryland-New York Province, superior of the Jesuit Mission in California, rector at Santa Clara College in California—before returning to Philadelphia in 1868.

Although Villiger's mandate was to develop a college, and Jesuits ordinarily did not organize parishes, one of his first conclusions—"our colleges must always have a church attached to them"—was that its growth depended on raising an associated church and congregation. So in five months he built a chapel and clergy residence, and by December 1868 had established the New St. Joseph's parish. (The original parish, in Willing's Alley, still uses the appellation Old St. Joseph's.) Within three years in the fast-growing neighborhood, the congregation, now called the Church of the Holy Family, numbered more than 2,000.

While St. Joseph's College lingered downtown, and Villiger went about his pastoral duties, he thought of the Holy Family building as a prospective college chapel, merely blessing it rather than dedicating it. Five years after its opening, he paid $14,000 to Quaker landowners for a companion site at 17th and Stiles and completed a parish school building—he liked to call it the "Preparatory Department of St. Joseph's College"—by 1879.

That year the Sisters of Notre Dame were called to staff the school, and thirteen years later the Sisters, Servants of the Immaculate Heart of Mary, took over the teaching of the boys. (The Notre Dame sisters remained at the parish until 1951; the I.H.M. sisters have never left.)

Plainly a visionary—and, fortunately, a prolific fund-raiser as well—Villiger next pursued his dream of building a landmark church, one of his models no less than the legendary 16th century Church of the Gesu (the Italian word for Jesus) in Rome. The parish broke ground at the corner of 18th and Stiles in the late winter of 1879 and on December 2, 1888, Philadelphia's own Church of the Gesu was dedicated.

Finally, the next autumn, a handful of young men who formed the entire student body of St. Joseph's College convened in their new accommodations adjacent to the church. An official history of the college observed: "On this day, delayed through twenty long and orphaned years, the contrast was unescapable [sic] between the lofty, capacious church that had been building during this time and the little group of students that occupied just a few pews in it. Nevertheless, the College in its three earlier inaugurations had never enjoyed such magnificent surroundings nor such happy prospects." The new president of the college was Father Villiger.

As the years took their toll, a weary Villiger left the parish he had created and the college he had nurtured for a quieter teaching life in Maryland, then, finally, back to the Gesu where he would rest through the last months of his life. Shortly after his return, in November 1901, St. Joseph's College celebrated its 50th anniversary, and Philadelphia's Archbishop Patrick J. Ryan took note of the place Villiger held in the community:

> In the hierarchy of the Church, there are various grades, and among them the Archbishop stands very high; but there is a far higher order of Patriarchs, and tonight we have here a patriarch. I, like the clergy and yourselves, bow to do him all the honor which he deserves on a night like this. . . .

He has done great things in that half-century; many of them visible; built a glorious church and later on this grand institution; but these are only visible evidences of the invisible good that he has done—the souls that he has consoled, his sympathy and assistance to the broken-hearted, the encouragement of sinners who knelt at his confessional. Invisible work! That only God and His angels saw . . .

Almost exactly a year later, Villiger died, and a Philadelphia newspaper, *The Public Ledger*, reported, under a headline, "Last Honors Paid to Father Villiger—Thousands Attend Funeral at Church of the Gesu—Beloved Jesuit Is Laid Tenderly at Rest in Holy Cross Cemetery":

. . . the feelings of sorrow felt by a congregation of probably more than three thousand persons. Many more, unable to obtain accommodations within, stood outside the edifice. Rarely has such a touching and impressive scene been witnessed in a church in this city.

The seeds that Villiger had sown flourished after his departure. At its height, not long after Villiger's death, parish membership was estimated at 20,000 people, including some of the city's important politicians and businessmen, leading a scholar to call it "one of the city's most prominent" parishes. It fostered dozens of religious societies, choirs, and clubs, providing its community with cradle-to-grave religious and social activities. For a few years the parish could afford to provide tuition for its children at St. Joseph's College. The congregation built a five-story rectory that became home to more than fifty Jesuit priests and scholastics.

As it prospered, the Church of the Gesu retained its working-class Irish roots, welcoming immigrants to the New World and preparing them to thrive in it. Even before Villiger's death, however, Philadelphia began to feel crowded to the more prosperous among the parishioners, who moved into the ring of suburbs growing rapidly around the center city. North Philadelphia, almost suburban when the Gesu was founded, soon was plainly a part of what came to be known as the inner city.

In a sense, the people of North Philadelphia served by the church were no different in the late 20th century than they had been a century earlier—working class or struggling class, trying to make ends meet, seeking education for their children as a stepping stone to a better life. But they were different in one critical aspect: Rather than being predominantly Irish-American, they were predominantly African-American.

The transition of this neighborhood from largely white to largely black followed a pattern like that in other parts of Philadelphia or in dozens of other cities across the United States: A few blacks (or another minority) move into a neighborhood, a few whites (of one ethnic group or another) move out; the numbers each way increase, until a "tipping point" is reached, after which the rate of change accelerates and the area becomes nearly all minority.

The clashes between ethnic whites and African-Americans in American cities throughout the 20th century is well enough known to require no detailed exposition here. Among cities, Philadelphia was a not untypical case, and among ethnic groups, the Irish were not untypical. But to understand what the Gesu parish represented, and what the Gesu School now represents, one must consider the relationship between Irish and blacks over the last half of the century.

Context is provided by the Philadelphia-born scholar Clark in his book, *Erin's Heirs: Irish Bonds of Community*:

> It was not so much that the Irish were more racist than other Americans. In fact, a good case could be made that they

were less so. The central consideration in the matter is that for most of the nation's history, the Irish, like the blacks, were steeped in the miseries at the bottom of the country's social system. Like blacks, they were assigned to the least desirable jobs, housing, and living conditions in most communities through the 19th century. Lack of education, competition for employment, and the social inflammation that derives from being frustrated and exploited deeply troubled both groups. The groups being placed so close together in big city slums resulted in a long history of combat and hostility.

Southern blacks had moved north in significant numbers to take factory jobs during World War I, and a similar outburst of northern migration occurred in World War II, in Philadelphia and other industrial centers. As more and more blacks arrived in the 1950s to join families and friends, the black population of Philadelphia increased from 378,000 to 535,000 during that single decade, which "changed the ethnic geography of the city," according to Clark:

> The slum and mill districts that had first been the homes of the Irish and that had then mingled Irish, Jews, Italians, and others beginning in the 1890s, were now dominated by blacks. . . . The buildings had been used and abused for a century, and there were no family funds to renovate them. They crumbled and were bulldozed, and much of North Philadelphia became a wasteland of cleared lots and abandoned wreckage inhabited by the crippled, the hunted, and the haunted. In the outlying areas of the city, big new Irish parishes had arisen, and their residents were largely contemptuous of the blacks who had taken over the "old neighborhoods."

The great Irish parishes of North Philadelphia—among them St. Michael's, St. Francis Xavier, St. Elizabeth's, Most Precious Blood, Our Lady of Mercy, St. Malachy's, and Gesu—were losing large numbers of their longtime members and gaining only small numbers among the new black residents; and tension often existed among parishioners of different races.

Actually, tension had existed for a considerable time. As early as the Great Depression, when things were tough for everybody, the arrival of a relatively small number of blacks was significant enough to provoke racist action. In his book, *Parish Boundaries: The Catholic Encounter with Race in the Twentieth-Century Urban North*, Notre Dame historian John T. McGreevy described the formation in 1936 of the Gesu Parish Neighborhood Improvement Association. Led by Father James Maguire, an Irish-born priest who lived in the Gesu rectory, its stated goal was to "keep and bring into the parish respectable home-owners and tenants and to prevent the further influx of undesirables into the neighborhood."

No one had any trouble understanding which was which by Maguire's measure. The Association kept track of housing vacancies and tried to find the "right" kind of newcomers to fill them, encouraged "appropriate" businesses, and discouraged housing speculators.

In sharp contrast to Maguire and his like stood parishioners like Anna McGarry, daughter of an Irish immigrant, who had devoted herself to interracial understanding since the early 1930s. Refusing to sell her home to blockbusting real-estate agents, McGarry, a World War I widow, was quoted as saying, "I believed that my husband had given his life to protect democracy, but here in my own neighborhood I saw actions that nullified his sacrifice."

McGarry and others, including Jesuit intellectuals, welcomed blacks into their neighborhoods and their churches and helped organize the Philadelphia Catholic Interracial Council. In the decade of the 1950s, with fewer than one in ten families living on all-white blocks, the Gesu church had become deeply concerned with the housing, welfare, and educational needs of the neighborhood's newer residents.

In 1945, for the first time, the Gesu parish school opened its doors to black children.

Just as important, physically and symbolically, the Jesuits literally held their ground at the elite St. Joseph's Prep. St. Joseph's College, which had been the *raison d'etre* for the formation of Gesu parish, moving from downtown to North Philadelphia in 1868, had run out of space again by 1927 and established a new campus on the northwest edge of Philadelphia. But "the Prep," which had been under pressure since the early 1950s to move toward its increasingly suburban student body, instead chose to recruit hard in the city and developed scholarships for minority boys.

A turning point came in 1965 when a fire severely damaged the school. It would have been excusable then for the Jesuits to evacuate their prep school. Instead, they embarked on a major financial campaign that produced its current modern structures; to this day, the Prep continues to expand in its home next to the Gesu church.

Whatever the attitudes, the Catholic population was unmistakably changing. Not just in the Philadelphia archdiocese, of course. A 1999 story in the *Philadelphia Inquirer* reported that Chicago had closed seventy-nine parishes since 1982, Detroit closed thirty-five parishes in the late 1980s, and from 1992 to 1994 Pittsburgh merged 163 of its 333 parishes into fifty-six and closed thirty-nine churches.

In 1997, only about one-third of the 1.35 million Catholics in the southeastern Pennsylvania archdiocese lived in the city of Philadelphia, a drop of nearly 25% from 1980. During those same years, the Catholic population of suburban Montgomery,

Chester, and Bucks counties rose by 27%, from 450,000 to 570,000. In the fifteen parishes surrounding Gesu in North Philadelphia, the number of Catholics dwindled from 54,000 in 1970 to 25,000 in 1991.

The racial make-up of the area had obviously changed drastically in the post-war decades. At the time of the Gesu suppression in 1993, Temple University researchers, studying an area within a one and one-quarter mile radius of the school, estimated that 95 per cent of the approximately 16,000 residents were African-American. (The Temple group also found that nearly half of those 25 years or older had not graduated from high school, 50 per cent of the households lived below the poverty level, and unemployment was about 20 per cent.)

As white Catholics moved away from the inner-city parishes, and African-Americans, mainly, replaced them, the change in the neighborhoods was not merely the succession of working-class and middle-class families by those struggling with a lack of education and blatant discrimination; it was also the fact that the new residents were usually not Catholic. Some African-Americans were Catholic and had been for generations, like Byron McCook's family, but they were more likely to be Baptist or African Methodist Episcopal or Pentecostal. The Gesu church was hit as hard as any: a parish that had counted some 5,000 members as recently as the 1930s, a parish that had once needed seven masses every Sunday, now could count only about 300 members.

The process that led to the closing of Gesu and other parishes in various parts of the five-county archdiocese—what the cardinal called "cluster planning"—began in 1991. It continued for about eighteen months, including pastors, lay representatives from the parishes, and administrators from archdiocesan headquarters in Center City—"222" as it is known for the street address.

In North Philadelphia, the archdiocese appeared to want to consolidate five parishes into two and close all schools except the two affiliated with those parishes. "The archdiocese does not run a school unless it is attached to a parish," said its secretary of Catholic education. The pastors and lay leaders wanted to save four parishes or at least three, and certainly four schools. "We wanted to maintain as many of the parishes as possible so that parishioners would not think of themselves as uprooted in a dying church," said someone who attended most of the meetings.

Although the process was said by the archdiocese to be collegial, it became clear before long to the North Philadelphians that archdiocesan administrators would stick to their plans. An internal memorandum written by an administrator for the Jesuit Province of Maryland said: "Most [parishioners] understand that something like this had to happen. What disturbs many people is the decision process. There had been discussion for eighteen months, but for seventeen of them the archdiocese spoke only in generalities, and specifically denied that the process was about parish closings and consolidations. Only in the last month did the discussion move to specifics with little time for discussion of those specifics."

Father Bur, the last pastor of Gesu parish, remembers with intense pain the experience of a decade ago: "Session after agonizing session the cardinal's representatives tried mightily to get two or three pastors and their congregations to surrender to their reasoning. Each congregation continued to hold dearly to its model of survival. . . .

"After cajoling and pressuring us for a decision according to his model, the cardinal knew he was not going to succeed in getting us to make the decision, and he finally took the bull by the horns and imposed his solution. . . . The change at Gesu was dramatic. There would be no more parish, but the cardinal wisely asked the Jesuits and the I.H.M. sisters to continue to keep the school open as a private Catholic school."

When the parish leaders were informed of the decision, in a closed meeting at 222, Bur was sitting with Father Jack McNamee, the pastor of St. Malachy's Church, which was to accept the Gesu parishioners. McNamee was astonished that his parish survived. "I'm not used to winning," he said.

The two priests decided to walk the mile back to North Philadelphia together to clear their heads and to consider how to organize the transition. As it happened, not that many people, perhaps half the Gesu congregation at most, accepted the forced transfer. "We lost a lot of our parishioners to the Catholic faith," said Byron McCook. "Some went to Baptist or Methodist churches." Did you feel let down? "Oh, yes. We didn't think it was a decision of God. More a decision of man."

"Many of the parishioners dragged themselves only with great reluctance to St. Malachy's," said Bur, "and grumbled about their perceptions of a poor welcome. Others vowed never to set foot in St. Malachy's and now belong to non-Catholic organizations." Bur remembered that as a boy his family and their neighbors had once been instructed to leave a parish in which they had invested many caring years and transfer to a newly established parish. "We made the transition obediently," he said. Now, "no one practiced the obedience willingly practiced in my childhood."

On June 27, 1993, the final parish mass was celebrated in the Church of the Gesu. It was reported in the *Inquirer*:

> They came yesterday from around the corner and as far away as Florida. . . . And they gathered to cry, to laugh, to rehash memories and, for some, to express uncertainty about Catholicism in North Philadelphia.
>
> . . . "My mother and father raised 13 children and were 37 years in the parish," said Rita Driscoll, who lived in Lawndale. "We all went to school here. All five girls got married here. I hate to see it close. I understand why it's closing, but it's very sad." . . .

Gesu's pastor, the Rev. George Bur, urged congregants to be thankful for memories and to keep an open mind about the consolidation.

. . . "Even if we disagree with the decision, we will not be a spiteful people."

Gerri Fitzgerald, a member of Gesu since 1979, held her emotions in check until the point at which congregants extended handshakes of peace with one another. Then the retired teacher began to sob. "I feel like I'm losing my family," Fitzgerald said.

The new pastor for the combined churches, the Rev. Jack McNamee, currently at St. Malachy's, yesterday tried to assure his new flock that "whatever relief or joy I feel at surviving the closings is chastened by the reality of the larger responsibility. . . . We all know how precarious and fragile life is in North Philadelphia. We've got to continue the work. We've just got to do it."

"Without the schools," Bur said, "I would judge the whole endeavor at consolidation as a disaster for the mission of the church in North Philadelphia. Thanks be to God: The children give us a mission that continues to engage hundreds of volunteers and continues to win support from outside the community."

The children. Thanks be to God.

The Many Faces of Gesu School

"All the pieces are in place. There isn't one part of their social, emotional, religious, or academic needs that is not addressed. (Gesu is) providing a truly academic atmosphere for the children — it's very clear that there is a strong academic thrust — but it's very clear that this is a school that is going to treat you like family."

— Gail Avicolli

(*top*) At the beginning of the 2003-2004 school year, Gesu kicked off its 10th anniversary as an independent Catholic school with a day-long Block Party in front of the school.

(*above*) Gesu's choir sings songs of celebration at a party for the completion of the Millennium Campaign in 1996

(*top*) Gesu opens the Church of the Gesu every June for the commencement ceremony, which brings together hundreds of family members.

(*above*) A collaborative effort between the Arthur Ashe Youth Tennis Center and Gesu students. Gesu students are afforded many extra-curricular opportunities ranging from golf and fencing to dragon boating and drama club.

(*top*) George W. Bur, S.J. accepts a donation from John Backe, President of Backe Communications, to establish the Writing Program at Gesu.

(*above*) Daryl Shore, '94 at his high school graduation with Gesu principal Sr. Ellen T. Convey, I.H.M. Daryl subsequently graduated from Emory University in Atlanta.

(*top*) Interior view of the Church of the Gesu, which, at its peak in the early Twentieth Century, hosted seven Masses every Sunday to accommodate all of its parishioners.

(*above*) The Sisters, Servants of the Immaculate Heart of Mary celebrated their 110th anniversary at Gesu School in the spring of 2001. From 1891 to 1951, the I.H.M. sisters taught only the boys at Gesu, while the Sisters of Notre Dame taught the girls. In 1951, the I.H.M. sisters took over the education of both the boys and the girls.

(*above*) Gesu chaplain Fr. Neil Ver'Schneider, S.J. with Gesu youngsters. With the reassignment of George W. Bur, S.J. to the Jesuit community at St. Joseph's University, Fr. Ver'Schneider becomes the lone Jesuit at Gesu School.

Religious & Church

(*top*) Fr. George W. Bur, S.J. with Fr. James Devereux, S.J.. As provincial of the Province of Maryland, Society of Jesus and Georgetown University board member, he encouraged fellow Georgetown board member Win Churchill to visit and get involved with Gesu School in the late 1980s.

(*above*) The Gesu principal Sr. Ellen T. Convey, I.H.M. at Gesu commencement ceremony.

(*top*) Win Churchill and George W. Bur, S.J. with Gesu kindergartners. They had been students at St. Joe's Prep together before reuniting thirty years later, at Fr. Jim Devereux's encouragement.

(*above*) Gesu Chairman Win Churchill with Gesu President Christine Beck and Gesu Trustee John J.F. Sherrerd

(*top*) Gesu Trustee and Millennium Campaign Co-Chair Mark Solomon and Gesu Trustee Daryl I. Shore, '94 with Symposium panelist Dr. Eugene Rivers

(*above*) Gesu Trustees Leif Beck and H. Scott Miller

(*top*) Gesu Trustee, parent, and longtime Church of the Gesu parishioner Byron McCook chats with former Gesu president and Church of the Gesu pastor Fr. George W. Bur, S.J. at Gesu's 10th Anniversary Block Party.

(*above*) Gesu Trustee and Children Succeeding Chair Ralph W. Saul with wife Bette. Children Succeeding raised more than $4 million for Gesu, allowing many new educational opportunities for Gesu students.

(*top*) Gesu pre-kindergartners listen during storytime. Pre-kindergartners came to Gesu for the first time in 1993.

(*above*) Gesu 8th graders critique each other's work in writing class, made possible by a grant from Backe Communications.

(*above*) All Gesu students enjoy art classes, which were made possible by funds raised through the Children Succeeding Campaign.

(*left, center*) Gesu's counselor Sr. Patricia McGrenra, I.H.M. with the Gesu Girls Club, a community-service oriented club for Gesu girls in 5th through 8th grades.

(*left, below*) Gesu maintains a heavy emphasis on literacy among all its students; a Gesu 7th grader buries his nose in a book.

(*top*) 8th grade teacher and leader of Gesu's peer mediation program Eilise Moran with neighborhood children at Gesu's 10th Anniversary Block Party

(*above*) Choir director and music teacher H.L. Ratliff with eager students

Teachers

(*above*) 2nd grade teacher Nora DeCarlo has fun with 4th grade boys teacher Christopher Harris at Gesu's 10th Anniversary Block Party

(*left*) 7th grade teacher Melinda Barno encourages one of her students with his assignment.

(*above*) Gesu kindergarten teacher Laura Ann Hood and one of her students greet each other in the morning.

(*right*) 2nd grade teacher Nora DeCarlo has taught at Gesu for more than thirty years.

(*top*) Churchill Challenge contributor James Kim with his wife Agnes visit the Kim Technology Center at Gesu School.

(*above*) Win Churchill with Gesu Trustee Dr. Anne Hubbard of the Hubbard Family Foundation, the fifth Churchill Challenge donor. The Churchill Challenge raised $5 million in endowment dollars for Gesu School.

(*top*) Win Churchill thanks Millennium Campaign Co-Chairs Mark Solomon and Peter Miller for a successful campaign. The Millennium Campaign, which raised $1.7 million, was Gesu's first major fundraising initiative as an independent Catholic school.

(*above*) Win Churchill and Gesu Trustee Jay Sherrerd share a laugh at the formal announcement of the Churchill Challenge. Jay and his wife Kathy were the first to accept Churchill's challenge for five donors each to donate $1 million for Gesu's endowment.

Symposium

(*top*) Gesu's first annual Symposium on Inner-City Education included former U.S. Secretary of Education William J. Bennett (third from left), Tim Russert of NBC News (fifth from right), and Joe Klein, author of *Primary Colors* (third from right).

(*above*) John J. DiIulio, political scientist and Gesu trustee, created the Gesu Symposium in 1997 and has moderated it every year.

Chapter X

'Wholeness, Joy, Community, Forgiveness'

"... there is a hope that education and opportunity will enhance the essential strength of the black community and make those strengths more available to a nation and a world that needs them."

George Bur grew up in a grand, old-fashioned Irish-Catholic family, but he has spent most of his adult life working in African-American communities. As he and I discussed the Gesu School's North Philadelphia neighborhood (which is described in the following chapter), I asked him to reflect on his relationships in those communities, the similarities and differences among people he has known. Here is his elegant response:

> Though it wasn't so apparently unusual to me as a child or even a teen-ager, I come from a traditional and even strict Catholic family. Over the years, however, the family, through suffering and change, began to be more open to the variety of ways in which people choose to live their lives.
>
> My mother in her sixties would quietly lobby for the divorced and remarried to participate fully in the church. My father once told me that the culture had changed so much that it could make sense for a young couple to live together before marriage. (Both of those things were certainly not part of their own upbringing, and, I suppose, are things that Catholic bishops might quietly condone nowadays!) To their dying day my parents continued to organize their social life around church events, prayed daily, attended Mass several times a week, and were generous to the church.
>
> As I engaged in my own ministry, the variety of ways in which peoples and their cultures express their faiths became more and more present to me. The joke, for example, about Irish Alzheimer's, that we forget everything but our grudges, was really not a joke in my grandmother's family. It was reality; the Irish in that generation told us that it was better to forget entirely a family member who had abandoned the family or the faith.
>
> In the black community, on the other hand, Catholic or not, the worse grudges are always subject to at least grudging

forgiveness. More than once in the black community I offici-ated at funerals of men who had abandoned their families, but, when they became terminally ill, the family rallied around, took care of them, and buried them properly.

I have come to believe that faith communities of peo-ple of Irish and northern European extraction need to rub shoulders with the faith expressed by African-American and Latino cultures. Religious orders like the Jesuits and the I.H.M. sisters make this happen within their own membership because of the variety of ministries which they undertake.

But because of the racial and economic segregation in everyday America, I suspect the old statistic is still true: Sunday morning at eleven is the most segregated hour in the week. I experience this segregation myself in many Philadelphia churches though it is rare now for a Catholic to worship in a congregation which is officially ethnic.

Gesu School is one of the hundreds of schools that Catholic religious orders are sponsoring in the poor minority communi-ties of our country. Educating these students is one way to create a healthier integrated climate. The considerable energy that the Catholic church is expending in these efforts will not necessarily show itself in the Catholic church pews on Sunday morning, because so many of our students are not Catholic and not even churched. But there is a hope that education and opportunity will enhance the essential strengths of the black community and make those strengths more available to a nation and a world that needs them.

Black Catholics confidently made a list of those strengths in a document they published about fifteen years ago concern-ing church worship: Wholeness, Joy, Community, and Forgiveness. These are strengths that are easy to find in the stu-dent body and families of Gesu School. We white educators must be sensitive to them. We are blessed to have some experience and many black colleagues who, for the most part, protect us from the teaching and school-organizing mistakes that fail to build on these qualities.

Wholeness

Even in academic studies, we find our students more focused if their bodies and hearts and minds can be occupied in a holistic way. Hands-on learning activities are a must at Gesu School, imitating the combination of body movement and heartfelt prayer that is evident in African-American worship.

Joy

Generally our younger children exhibit this joy by their affection for the others in the school community. They are smiling and tactile. Sometimes this happens despite the lack of parental affection. Joy is not readily associated with our adolescents who are struggling to grow up in a culture alien to it. So we have to work hard at providing opportunities for the joy of running in track; for the joy of performing on the stage, or for the joy of reading and writing poetry. These joys just like those expressed in worship are the result of hard work and sometimes even suffering.

Community

So many of our school families teach us lessons about community, especially about the community of family. Grandparents and aunts and uncles raise the children abandoned by their parents. Troubled children are sometimes supported by an entirely different family. Gesu School teaches kids with both parents in jail or on the street. Gesu School teaches kids who live in close quarters because of house fires or evictions. But these children arrive at school most every day because some adults band together to make sure that they do. Such practices have their counterparts in the support systems built by the churches.

Forgiveness

The most difficult forgiveness for our children is the day-to-day forgiveness, forgiveness for the slights or insults or physical intrusions which occur every day. But there is a wide forgiveness of the world for their not being born into different circumstances. And I do not mean only the sentiment that Black is Beautiful. There is also a willingness to make the best of it despite the lack of a parent or the lack of material goods. This strength has its source in some long history that joins itself to the church at a more recent date.

So what return is made to those of us who teach each day at Gesu School? Whatever our own cultures offered us by way of wholeness, joy, community, and forgiveness, the experience here with our families and children enhances these qualities. For me, sometimes the experience places my own tradition in a poor light.

The experience certainly has colored my world vividly and strengthened my understanding of the depth and breadth of God's love. I wish nothing less for everyone in the minority to which I belong, we white American males, such a small percentage of the world's population.

Chapter XI

North Philadelphia

"... the Gesu has decided that America is a mission country, and North Central Philadelphia is a mission territory."

Cecilia Ross-Kent, a soft-spoken case worker for the Pennsylvania Department of Public Welfare, gets up about 5 a.m. at her home in Southwest Philadelphia, dresses for her professional day, and helps her son prepare for school. They leave home about 6:30 a.m. to take the 108 bus that stops just outside her house; if the 108 seems late, she and her son walk four blocks to take a different bus. They change buses twice, three rides in all, to reach Gesu about 7:30 a.m.

Sometimes Ross-Kent finds it necessary to ride the subway, which is faster, but she has a touch of arthritis and finds it difficult to go up and down stairs, so usually it's the bus. The third bus leaves her son and her near the school; she walks him to the building, then takes a fourth bus to her office near the 30th Street railroad station, about ten minutes away if the bus is on time. Usually she is at work by 8 a.m.

In the afternoon, she performs the whole trip in reverse, five days a week, nine months a year.

Ross-Kent is a mother of a Gesu boy and a mother of a girl who graduated from Gesu in 2000 and is now a student at West Catholic High School.

She is also a grandmother of three Gesu students. Since Ross-Kent's daughter, the mother of those children, is at work during the day, Ross-Kent's mother—the children's great-grandmother, who lives nearby—makes sure they are escorted to school and picked up. "If my mother comes to school, she just says her name," said Ross-Kent. "Sister Ellen knows to call my son and my grandchildren. She knows everybody's name. The whole theory of Gesu is, it's a whole village to raise a child."

Cecilia Ross-Kent exemplifies the constituency that Gesu exists to serve, in no small part because she exemplifies as well the dedication that its constituency offers every day to Gesu. It hardly needs saying that the fall and rise of the Gesu School is irrevocably tied to the evolution of North Philadelphia over the past century—and the momentous movement since the 1960s—so it is instructive to consider the state of the neighborhood today, its past and its possible future.

Among the constant presences in North Philly for more than a century have been the Church of the Gesu and the boys school that followed the Jesuits to the site, St. Joseph's Preparatory School. The Prep, which rebuilt itself from the ashes of a 1966 fire, occupies most of the block bordered by Thompson and Girard, 17th and 18th streets, the site purchased in the mid-19th century by Father Villiger. Besides its current facilities, it owns the building it once used for classes, now occupied by the Gesu School, and an adjoining building, once a home for Jesuit priests and brothers, now unused.

The Church of the Gesu, clad in burnt-orange brick, decorated with a dozen white columns and five red doors, stands between the modern Prep buildings on one side and on the other tiny houses across narrow 18th Street, some decrepit, a few rehabilitated. Glancing at the church's three-story façade, a casual viewer might not appreciate the masonry foundation and the walls, ten feet thick, eighty-four feet high, built just as masonry was giving way to steel—a building once described as "a triumph of architectural skill and daring."

Inside, the church shows itself off. The barrel-vaulted ceiling reaches 100 feet above the center aisle, held in place by the massive walls and a forest of oak beams. It is nearly the length of a football field from the entry doors to the baroque main altar, which is seventy-two feet high and thirty-six feet wide at its base. It might be the largest church in terms of cubic feet in all of Philadelphia, except perhaps the Catholic cathedral in Center City.

Chapels dedicated to St. Joseph and the Virgin Mary and altars dedicated to the Jesuit saints, Ignatius of Loyola and Francis Xavier, occupy the sides along with eight smaller chapels.

Statues, paintings, decorative art of all kinds adorn the walls and inlets. The wooden benches will seat more than 1,000 people; at its peak, this church needed six and seven masses on a Sunday to accommodate its parishioners. Now, without a parish, it holds no regular masses; the nearest parish church, St. Malachy's, where the former Gesu congregation was assigned, is eight blocks away.

Lacking air-conditioning and not well-heated, the building is the site of a dozen or so masses and other celebrations for Prep students in a year, and a half-dozen for Gesu students including graduation. "The little ones, they sit here and look around, they think they're at the Vatican," said Father Bur with a smile.

Active houses of worship of one kind or another enliven the neighborhood. Near the dormant Gesu lie a number of important Protestant churches, the 10th Memorial Baptist Church, the 2nd Pilgrim Baptist Church, the African Methodist Episcopal Zion Church at 19th Street.

A short distance north of the Gesu School, on Diamond Street, stands the Episcopal Church of the Advocate, a noted Gothic Revival structure dating to the late 19th century. Once a house of worship for upper-crust Philadelphians who lived in elegant brownstones and Victorians on the wide streets nearby, it has served a comfortable African-American community since before World War II. It was at the Church of the Advocate that the first eleven women Episcopal priests were ordained, and the church hosted important Black Power meetings in the 1960s and '70s, earning it designation as a National Historic Landmark.

Not much farther away, at 20th and Lehigh, is the site where the Philadelphia Athletics and Philadelphia Phillies once played, first called Shibe Park then Connie Mack Stadium. Now the old ball yard is gone, replaced by something that looks like a basketball arena; but it too is a church, the Deliverance Evangelistic church, bordered by a shopping center that the church owns and a neighborhood that displays the substantial benefits of the church's influence.

Much of North Philly, and certainly the area around Gesu, is dotted with what are usually known as "storefront churches," mainly former houses, which are each renovated into a gathering place with a sign outside announcing a church. Thanks to the U.S. Constitution, there is no license required for a minister, the principal challenge being that one can gather a congregation. Most are not affiliated with national religious organizations. Longtime residents say that many of the storefront churches near Gesu are led by people newly arrived in the area who brought with them ready-made congregations.

The housing stock of the neighborhood, depending how widely "neighborhood" is defined, varies enormously in quality. Many homes in the school's immediate area are simple three-story buildings, two windows wide, in all levels of maintenance, some thoughtfully cared for, more of them tacky, others abandoned and boarded up. Vacant lots abound. Spread over a square mile or so not far from the school exist former mansions and brownstones, also in various states of repair, usually converted to apartments or even single-room-occupancy buildings.

This is truly the "Gesu neighborhood" because about three out of four of its students live within three miles of the school. In 2003-04, 82% of Gesu families applied for financial aid. Of those, nearly one in five children live in families with annual incomes below $10,000, nearly half in families with annual incomes below $25,000, and nearly three-quarters in families with annual incomes below $35,000. About 70% of the students come from households with a single adult; many are being raised by grandparents and in one case by a great-grandmother.

If someone can be called the "matriarch" of the neighborhood around Gesu – and an exemplar of what's positive about the neighborhood – it would be Mrs. Katie Robinson. No one calls her Mrs. Robinson. No one calls her Katie either. Everyone calls her Miss Katie, a note of friendly informality yet a note also of respect.

In her childhood Miss Katie alternated between the *de jure* segregated schools of her native North Carolina and the *de facto* segregated schools of North Philadelphia where her extended family lived. She met her husband while he was stationed at Fort Bragg, North Carolina, and introduced him to Philadelphia after his Korean War service. Born into a religious Baptist family, Miss Katie sampled several Protestant churches in Philadelphia, "looking for Southern hospitality, but Northerners didn't have it. I'm sorry to say it, but they just didn't have it."

Her first exposure to Catholicism came as a little girl, tagging along with her grandmother who did cleaning for the Little Sisters of the Assumption. As a young woman, Miss Katie's curiosity was piqued by a Catholic friend and, "being the inquisitive type," she decided one day to ring the doorbell at a church. She remembered seeing a lot of priests around and a lot of receptionists, finally gaining an audience with a young priest who gave her books to study and offered her instruction five days a week.

"The next thing I know, I'm grabbing the children every day to go to instruction, and asking my husband if he minded raising the children in the Catholic faith. He said it was no problem for him. So that was the beginning of my journey in Gesu, and I've been there ever since."

Baptized a Catholic in 1955, Miss Katie was a self-described "eager beaver" volunteer in a parish busy with community affairs. All of her five children attended Gesu, several of her twenty-three (and counting) grandchildren attend now, and, she hopes, some of her three (and counting) great grandchildren will.

In 1962 a priest told her about a house for sale on Thompson Street, across from the Gesu School. She and her husband bought it for $4,500, "big money at that time, $50 a month after the down payment," and she has lived there ever since. Miss Katie has seen a lot from that house at the corner of 18th and Thompson streets, seen a neighborhood that has gone down and up hill.

She thinks the early 1960s were the worst time, with gang wars commonplace on her side of a major North Philly thoroughfare, Girard Avenue. "My kids were not allowed to go to Girard Avenue unless I was with them. We lived through that terror." The turf wars gradually eroded, partly through community effort and partly because the gangs wore themselves out.

More recently, drugs have become the disease of choice, but Miss Katie thinks her neighborhood sometimes gets a bad rap. "They talk about [what happens here] more than they do [about the suburbs], but in the afternoon, you can see white people, blacks, Asians, Hispanics, you name it, they don't even live in the neighborhood," arriving to make their purchases.

Byron McCook, a generation younger than Miss Katie, remembers the streets around Gesu as so ugly, so dangerous that the neighborhood today seems almost comfortable by comparison. "When I was a child going to Gesu, we had gangs, turf fights. I lived on the other side of the tracks, the other side of Girard Avenue, and crossing those tracks was risky. In my area, the main gang was called the Moroccos, and [near the school] was the Seybert Street gang. There would be hundreds and hundreds of kids; they would walk through the streets [carrying] bottles, knives, bricks.

"Fortunately I was not a member of any gang. Not getting drafted into a gang was a challenge. When they got to know who

I was, and to find out who my dad was, they began to leave me alone. [It was the same] with my older brother. We were able to receive at least that much respect, not for who we were, but for who our parents were."

McCook's mother was a licensed practical nurse and then a stay-at-home mom. His late father, a tailor by trade, was an important figure in the Gesu parish and an African-American political leader, "beneficial in helping a lot of families with problems." It was a stable family, and it remains so. McCook's mother still lives in the house in which she raised her children, about four blocks south of Gesu; Byron lives with his family three doors down the block.

With those parents, who gave him a solid home and a firm religious grounding, McCook attended Gesu when it was a parish school and went on to graduate from Temple University with a double major in computer and information science and business administration, then earned a master's degree in education from Rosemont College. He is now director of technology for a suburban Philadelphia school district.

But he has never left the neighborhood in which he grew up, even as it swung back and forth through the years. Although white families still lived there when McCook was a small child, by the 1970s nearly all had left for the suburbs. Then, beginning in the '80s and more rapidly in the '90s, white families began to move back onto some of the blocks in the process called gentrification, rehabilitating classic Victorian mansions and Federal townhouses, taking advantage of the proximity to Center City.

McCook concedes that violent crime still exists in the neighborhood—car break-ins, house burglaries—but insists that the toll has fallen drastically. Further, he agrees with Katie Robinson that most of the criminals come from outside the community, attracted by a drug culture that plays a far more important role in the area now than during his childhood.

McCook finds his neighborhood easier to live in than when he was growing up because "the majority of people [especially a few blocks south of the school] are working-class people with real jobs, homeowners, citizens who contribute, people who are raising their children. What I find interesting is the number of guys I grew up with, some who were in gangs, some not, who have really turned out to be productive people."

In his childhood days, McCook said, those friends were raised mostly by a single parent or grandparents; they knew what it was like "to go without, to feel left out, rejected. Now that they are parents, they recognize that they have a lot of control over their children, and they want them to have opportunities they didn't have."

Perhaps the most hopeful example of the parental—and neighborhood—evocation of the past and the present is Gesu's annual Beef and Beer cabaret. Scheduled on a Saturday near St. Patrick's Day, it is first a reminder of the parish's Irish roots and the bingo games that were major social events and fund-raisers decades ago. When the state changed the law in the 1970s to ban big prizes, and most of the Irish had already left the parish, bingo lost much of its popularity.

So in the late '70s, Byron McCook's father, Sylvester McCook, invented Beef and Beer as a neighborhood party that would produce money for the parish. The first year the parish sold 200 tickets at $5 apiece. Now the school sells more than 1,000 tickets at $20 each, the crowd almost overflowing an auditorium at St. Joseph's Prep. It takes about fifty volunteers, including Miss Katie, to staff the party; a half-dozen of them work for days preparing thinly sliced roast beef *au jus* served on Kaiser rolls, all you can eat for five hours, plus keg beer.

Beef and Beer is the biggest fund-raising event of its type at the school, although sales of pizza, candy, and Florida fruit have been tried over the years. Someone once suggested an art auction, but someone else pointed out that to bid for art the guests would probably need at least $150 or $200, and most people in the neighborhood didn't have that kind of spending money available.

Father Bur is pleased with the neighborhood camaraderie fostered by Beef and Beer. (He once felt "a little uneasy" about the level of drinking, but the partygoers are careful and there hasn't been a problem in years.) He is particularly pleased that most of the school's teachers now attend; that wasn't always true, but staff friendships have grown in recent years. Gesu students are not invited.

Community events like Beef and Beer, sponsored by a Catholic school, deliver exactly the kind of message about the inner-city that the Catholic hierarchy is missing, said John DiIulio. He is a white man, a nationally recognized scholar, a Catholic, and in our first meeting, he stopped little short of outrage in judging the hierarchy's view of its role in urban America. "The Vatican does not consider America a mission country," DiIulio said. "Sub-Saharan Africa is a mission, but North Central Philadelphia is not a mission. Well, the Gesu has decided that America is a mission country, and North Central Philadelphia is a mission territory.

"While they may not be dying, as priests in Africa are with AIDS victims, priests like Father Bur will die serving those children in that community. They're not running for pope, or bishop, they're not interested in politics. What you have are people who are selflessly dedicated to the well-being of children. Which is another way of saying, they love these children, they love that neighborhood, and they view it as their responsibility. Nobody else is making this possible, not corporations, or government. But [they say], you and me, we'll do it. That's their mission territory. They're missionaries.

"Closing parishes and not treating cities as mission places is a mistake. It's a missed opportunity because the Catholic church in American could have Gesu schools everywhere. They could if they would only realize that rather than building warehouse, K-Mart-like Catholic schools out in the suburbs, to serve populations de-urbanized, they could excite more of those people about their Catholic faith by challenging them to come back into the city, not to live, but to come back in the city to worship, to come back in the city to volunteer. The reason the Catholic church is having problems with its flock is because it's not confronting them fully with the obligations of Catholic social thought.

"I did a prayer breakfast out in Valley Forge [a few months] ago. We had 600 people there, mainly Protestants from all over the Delaware valley, to hear me and an African-American Baptist preacher from North Philly. We made a call to obedience, Christianity in the city. We got 400-some postcards after that saying, 'where do I go, what do I do, how do I sign up?'

"You challenge suburban Catholic parishes and congregations to have sister schools, adopt schools in the city. You seek, you find. I have yet to have an experience of asking and not getting. The problem is, I shouldn't be doing the asking. It should be the institutional Catholic church, the bishops.

"Make a year, 2004, the year of the urban mission. You'll have more young people coming back into the church. You'll have more young Catholics coming into the church, you'll have more older Catholics returning to the church. People love to do witness. What they don't understand is, the 9:30 or 11 o'clock mass, it's a pain in the ass to park, a guy [in the pulpit] goes on about something or other, the air-conditioner is broken, and we need $1,200 to fix it. You're wasting this.

"[The church] needs to bring forward people like George Bur to tell their story, to bring forward people who are doing this kind of work in the Catholic community. Closing the Gesu parish, the Gesu School, was, just to take it from a leadership and marketing standpoint, inane. The school was going to close; now it's a great success. Everybody's for it. What do you think, it's just something in the water supply of that particular piece of North Central Philadelphia? [It's because] there are people like George.

"There's Father [Arthur] Taraborelli at St. Thomas Aquinas. You have an Italian priest, and his brother [a layman], at 18th and Morris in Philadelphia—almost entirely African-American students, like Gesu except it's [an official part of the archdiocese]. What used to be a convent is now a home for battered Asian women. Only in America: Italian 'priests.' African-American kids. Battered Asian women. You can't make this up.

"Meanwhile, twenty miles out, in the outer 'burbs, there's ongoing construction, build the Catholic religion, McMansions. This is a problem. It's as big a problem for the church as any of the pedophile priests. This is a real long-term, secular trend problem that's solvable. How is it solvable? The way the problem's always been solved in the history of the church: by having a Catholic reawakening that calls people back to faith that works, calls people back to racial reconciliation on behalf, in this case, of the inner-city poor. It's time to get off our prophetic voice, get off our prophetic ass, and let's go. You do that, you call them, they come. You build it, they come. You close it, they vanish.

"That's the decision. [People say] 'I left, you closed it, that's it. You've legitimized my decision. Now I've got 400 channels, I can watch kickboxing live from the Philippines eight hours a day if I want. I never have to see or do anything; I lock my doors; I drive past the [old] neighborhood. Who cares? Oh, my grandmother used to live there. So what, she's dead. You're gone, this parish is closed. Does anybody live there now? Yes. Those people, those people and their kids.'"

One of those people is Ross-Kent, who grew up in North Philadelphia, third oldest of nine children, their father working nights in computer operations for the Federal government, their mother working days packing catalogues for a mail-order company. After high school, she attended Pennsylvania State University at its flagship campus in State College for two years, holding several jobs to support herself, before finishing college in Philadelphia. While in college she had her first child.

Until a few years ago, Ross-Kent lived in North Philly and her younger daughter attended Gesu for three years. When Ross-Kent remarried and moved to South Philly with her husband, a bus driver, her daughter was enrolled in a public middle school. It was a disaster.

"When you take your child from Gesu, it's very hard to adjust," Ross-Kent said. [In the middle school] "she couldn't adjust to the lack of control in the classroom, couldn't adjust to the different attitudes of the teachers. When I talked to the teacher, she only knew the children by their seat numbers. I said, 'If you only know her by seat number, then you don't know my child.' It took me two and one-half months to get to the vice-principal; it took me six months to meet with the principal."

Ross-Kent waited until her son Shawn grew old enough to enter kindergarten, then enrolled him at Gesu and transferred her daughter Angela back. Angela had cried for three years, Ross-Kent said, and soon she was happy again. The three-hour daily commute was worth every minute.

Not at once. When Angela returned to Gesu from her public school, she was behind her Gesu classmates. "I was really concerned," Ross-Kent said. "I didn't know what to do. I didn't want to put her back in the public school, but I didn't want her to be a complete failure in everything. We would be up until 11 o'clock every night." Angela's teacher and Sister Ellen grasped the problem quickly and arranged to tutor her every day for nearly three months until she caught up. "The teacher said to just be patient. She thought that Angela could do it, and she did." By the time she graduated, she had earned the highest GPA in her class and won a scholarship to West Catholic.

And the grandchildren. Ross-Kent remembers well the day a girl in her granddaughter's public school in North Philly pulled a knife on her. "The first thing a parent is concerned about is safety, the care they get," she said. "I didn't have the money, but we decided [my three grandchildren] had to be at Gesu." What about the extra tuition? "We've been able to get through. I pay what I can. $50 here, $50 there. I just thank the Lord it worked out for them."

Byron McCook is also thankful. Education, he contends, is the most important factor in the community's improvement over the past couple of decades. His immediate neighborhood, a few blocks south of Gesu, is clearly a safer and more substantial area than that around the school, but he is optimistic even about Gesu's neighborhood, thanks in part to the school itself. "There is a tremendous amount of respect from even the less fortunate members of society for this institution," he said. "The people born and raised in this community know about it, and those who come afterwards learn about it soon."

Miss Katie is ever hopeful. Some drug houses have been torn down, she said, replaced by townhouses, and not too far away the area is gentrifying. A growing number of young professionals take advantage of inexpensive real estate and turn their blocks into display cases of what the inner-city can again become. After all, Philadelphia is an old city, a pre-automobile city, and from the Gesu School it is a comfortable walk to Temple University and the Community College of Philadelphia, and a bracing walk to the office towers of Center City or the magnificent Philadelphia Museum of Art where visitors can climb the stairs Rocky Balboa did. "By 2010, or 2015," Miss Katie said, "this is going to be the showplace of Philadelphia."

Chapter XII

Teacher and Cheerleader

"When we got to the Lincoln Memorial . . . they started reading out loud the Gettysburg Address. Wow! Whew! . . . I got teary."

J ohn DiIulio has taught at Harvard, Princeton, and the University of Pennsylvania, co-authored an influential government textbook, and achieved academic renown as a political scientist. He became nationally known as the first director of President George W. Bush's Office of Faith-Based and Community Initiatives. He promised the administration six months of service and left his White House office for the last time on September 10, 2001. Now he is back teaching at Penn and serving as a trustee—and one of the chief cheerleaders—for the Gesu School.

It should not be surprising that DiIulio was brought into the Gesu fold by one of its well-connected supporters, in this case the retired insurance executive and philanthropist Ralph Saul, who as a Brookings Institution trustee knew him as a scholar there. When the school was in trouble, DiIulio suggested with a whimsical smile, "Father Bur did the 'Jesuitical thing' and found a Noah's Ark, Win Churchill, and this powerelite, corporate, interdenominational, interfaith board."

DiIulio has toiled regularly to raise money for the school, working the telephone, inviting prospective supporters to visit, "making sure Gesu is remembered." He has written articles about the school for Philadelphia newspapers, education journals, and the national political magazine *The Weekly Standard*. He is the fulcrum for the annual Gesu symposium, which brings nationally prominent educators, journalists, and religious and civic leaders to the school to discuss critical educational and political issues.

"I've worked with lots of places, religious, non-religious, over the last fifteen to twenty years, but Gesu is just at the top of my list, at the top of my heart—because of the incredible commitment manifest by Father Bur, by Sister Ellen, by the whole crew there. Also because of the smart way that they do what they do with the kids, and the results, which pretty much speak for themselves.

138

"But what I wanted to discover, as I became part of the Gesu extended family, was, what does it do, why is it effective, what is distinctive about it. I had to get closer, had to have something more than just 'some of our kids graduate from high school.' They said, 'come see it.'"

So he did.

*   *   *

"The way I resolved to get closer was to teach there for a semester in the spring of 1998—teaching American government to the 8ᵗʰ grade, two hours a week, twenty girls and twenty boys. I had been teaching American politics at Princeton for eleven years, at Harvard for three years before that. Sister Ellen told me quickly, I'd never really taught. Sister gave me all the rope I needed to hang myself.

"The thing I'm proudest of, the really great experience, was the textbook. I wrote the American government textbook with James Q. Wilson, my mentor at Harvard [now at UCLA]. I used the same textbook I had used at Princeton and Harvard with my Gesu kids. Not everybody got it at the same level, but every kid could read that textbook. That told me something about their literacy, about the strength of the reading program.

"The first three or four weeks it was a matter of gaining their trust, which is a complicated thing. About four weeks into the semester, the kids learned, 'Oh, you're coming back, it's not just a gig,' then you become part of them and they open up." DiIulio remembered a pivotal moment. "I was talking about the Constitutional convention, fifty-five men meeting in Philadelphia one summer, it was hot, they had fights. One of the kids said, 'Dr. D, you get fifty-five guys in Philly in the summer, you're going to have fights.'"

DiIulio assumed that the children would be particularly interested in civil rights, but early discussions were a dud. So he turned to local issues, starting with essays about the biggest problems in their neighborhoods. "The essays made your hair stand on end. Drug abuse, domestic violence, the whole range of things. Why can't the mayor solve those problems, they wanted to know. They thought that there's somebody who controls everything. That guy, whoever he is, he's going to take care of everything."

The children soon learned that in a city like Philadelphia the mayor has to deal with the city council, and nationally the president has to deal with Congress. "They saw that. They got it instantly. So there's a lot of guys who are involved in this thing, they're all pulling in different directions, nobody's really in charge. So they say, 'how do you get things done that way?'"

Now DiIulio found his segue back to civil rights. "We saw how, let's see, they couldn't get it through state governments, which were big segregationists; they couldn't get it through Congress at the national level because it was still dominated by a lot of those segregationist people. So where would you go. They went to the courts. The kids invented the strategy that Thurgood Marshall and the NAACP used—literally, I'm not kidding you—on their own.

"'Where we gonna go now? Can't go to Congress, got Strom Thurmond and his guys. Lyndon Johnson—isn't he the guy who signed the civil rights bill?—but he couldn't get too far ahead. The states can't do it. The states are the problem. Remember that picture of George Wallace standing there, and that man Nick Katzenbach in front of him, remember that? What are we gonna do? We're gonna go to court—the Supreme Court. That's what, we can get the Supreme Court.' That's exactly what they did, the kids.

"I mean, I've been teaching twenty years. I had wonderful students at Harvard, great students at Princeton, great students in these years at Penn. But those moments with the kids at Gesu . . .

"We took a class trip to Washington. As we were winding through the edges of DC, a couple of kids said, 'Dr. D, this is lousy, this is worse than Philadelphia.' I said, 'it cleans up, you'll see.' Their big thing was Planet Hollywood. So we did have lunch there."

And did a lot more: the tour that day crammed in the Washington Monument; the Supreme Court, "where they had to be quiet for a long time, which was hard"; the FDR Memorial, "which they really liked." The children ran all day; they hardly sat down.

"When we got to the Lincoln Memorial, they loved those steps, they were running up and down those steps. Finally I got up there [to the seated Lincoln]. First the girls, then the boys, they started reading out loud the Gettysburg Address." DiIulio pauses, sighs. "Wow! Whew! People stopped and stared. A bunch of kids. They can't be doing that. You can't make this up. In Hollywood they couldn't. It would be clichéd. I just remember walking up the steps, huffing and puffing, and I see them gathered. As I was approaching them, I got teary. It was unbelievable. They read the whole thing. And of course they had pictures. They must have taken a thousand pictures.

"Then [that spring] they graduated. That particular ceremony was special, a bonding experience for me, with the school, with those particular kids."

*   *   *

This teaching experience not only ranked among the highlights of his career, DiIulio said, but it also prepared him as an evangelist for Gesu: "Now I had an understanding of the way the school works, of the kids, what they look like and how they're doing. What the true strengths and needs of the place are. It made me more effective as a friend of the school, to help in development, to take this show on the road."

DiIulio helps in myriad ways, one of them quite direct: He and his wife established a scholarship in memory of Chris Georges, a student of his at Harvard and a former editor of the *Harvard Crimson*, who covered Congress for the *Wall Street Journal* until his death at the age of thirty-three.

Less direct but possibly more far-reaching is the annual Gesu Symposium on Inner-City Education, the first of which was held in the fall of 1997 with the theme "Faith-Based Education." Thanks to DiIulio's contacts, an elementary school in North Philly attracted an A-list of participants: Tim Russert, host of NBC's "Meet the Press," as moderator; William Bennett, the former U.S. secretary of education and Federal drug czar as well as a best-selling author; Joe Klein, a political journalist and author of the best-selling book *Primary Colors*; Jane Eisner, editorial page editor and former London bureau chief of the *Philadelphia Inquirer*; and Rev. Eugene Rivers, whose Dorchester, Massachusetts literacy program for black children is one of the nation's models.

An audience of several hundred gathered in the modest basement of Gesu, heard the school choir open the program with a *largo* hymn that evolved into finger-snapping gospel, and a welcome from Win Churchill who said, "This may seem an unlikely place for miracles, but we have 400 small miracles a day." Bennett said simply, "Schools like this save children's lives."

The 1998 symposium, "Do Faith and Vouchers Mix?" (obviously before the U.S. Supreme Court offered limited approval to vouchers in the spring of 2002), answered the question affirmatively as might have been expected from this panel. Bennett, who came to his second symposium, contended that what amounts to vouchers, that is, allowing individuals or families to use public funds at any educational institution, is accepted in day-care and pre-school programs and in higher education; the exceptions are in between, the elementary and secondary schools. "Choice works," he said. It "narrows the gap between rich and poor."

DiIulio argued that the voucher debate was not a question of giving public money to private schools but rather giving money to parents "for the education of the public."

*   *   *

Expanding on the subject in a discussion that he and I had, DiIulio observed that vouchers frequently become a punching bag for people who are itching for a wider argument. "Public schools have a lot of problems, urban public schools have a lot of problems, and we should try to continue to repair them," he said, "but why get into a situation where you have Sandy Feldman [president of the American Federation of Teachers] fighting Chris Whittle [chairman of Edison, Inc., the for-profit company that contracts to operate public schools] two out of three falls.

"As I learned in my seven months in Washington, some people are determined to have a fight whether or not there's anything to fight about. So we're going to have a fight about vouchers. The right wants to have a fight about vouchers, school choice, and privatization. That's a fight they want to have. If you don't want to fight, they're going to shadow box. The left, the traditionalists, the teachers unions, want to fight about more funding, this, that, or the other.

"They're going to have that fight whether or not you show up. You've got these people who are dancing around these issues. All you have to do is shove a few matches on that, poof, it goes right up.

"I have talked to people [in recent years] who are major figures in teachers unions around the country and talked to big funders of the pro-voucher movement. Behind closed doors in each case they say, of course we should [compromise]. But if we do that, we'll be admitting—fill in the blank: then we can't push for full choice or then we can't push for greater teacher pay. Nobody wants to solve the problem because that problem feeds the fight, feeds the funding, feeds the whole industry of people on both sides who have interests in keeping the problem alive.

"I think the difference in a place like Gesu is, they just want to solve the problem."

*   *   *

The 2001 symposium, following by less than two months the September 11 terrorist attack, began not with hymns as in prior years but with the Gesu choir singing "America" and "God Bless America." Welcoming remarks came from 7th grader Desmond Shannon who said he was writing a novel about a 7th grade boy. Desmond then offered a detailed plan for his own future: college at Georgetown, Temple, or Harvard, then law school, then, after he gets settled, "I want to meet the girl of my dreams and have two children, hopefully twins, a boy and a girl."

Everyone was conscious, obviously, of the 9/11 catastrophe. "The real weapon against terrorism is education," Churchill told the audience, "and its consequence, equal opportunity." Referring to Gesu as "the little school that could," DiIulio, who had left the Faith-Based Initiative on the day before the assault, said that for all the painful problems thrust upon the nation, we must "keep a light burning for these issues."

The issues facing this little school are not strictly educational, as DiIulio sees it; Gesu can serve in many ways: "A leadership model of service, a servant model of leadership. Father Bur, all the people there, see themselves as in service not just to the students in the school, but to that community.

"We should handle our problems up close and personal whenever possible. Make a local telephone call for help if we can't do it ourselves or in the neighborhood. Or make 'a long-distance call' for help if we need to, the way my grandmother did in the Great Depression. My grandmother in South Philly, they had a problem, called poverty. The church helped, but it couldn't help enough. They went to the Philadelphia City Hall, which didn't help. They went to Harrisburg, which was like a foreign country, who knew Harrisburg, and it didn't help. Help came from Mr. Roosevelt, who my grandmother lit a candle to every day.

"The idea wasn't, we're always going to be dependent on Mr. Roosevelt and the national government. But don't be allergic to government or any other institution. We have one common good. One common good—one common conception of personhood. Government should serve it. Corporations should serve it. The church should serve it. It's a partnership model."

This concept fortifies DiIulio's belief in "Catholic social teaching," and he sees a number of influential advocates. "I think President Bush is guilty of being a Catholic social-thought guy. He's justly accused by some of being that, because, good Methodist that he is, he's not entirely foreign to that teaching. You listen to what Hillary Clinton says these days on the subject; it's identical to what Bush says. Both Methodists are doing Catholic social teaching. I'm proud to have had a hand in each of those cases.

"But I didn't learn it by reading Catholic catechism. I learned it by observing the Gesu School and other things like it. It's one thing to read the sixteen documents of Vatican II, one thing to read the pope's encyclicals. It's another thing to see people like George and Ellen and those teachers and that choir showing up every day.

"You know, these kids are not easy to deal with on a daily basis. It's not every day a teacher arrives and says, 'Oh, I'm so happy.' It's hard work. It's a pain in the ass sometimes, but they keep coming back, because they have this commitment, and because they have a theory of the problem that has its practical aspects and has its moral aspects. So I think Catholic social teaching and social doctrine is still the most radical and the most true form of public philosophy available to us in any place or time. Whenever it gets followed, it works; when it's deviated from, it doesn't work."

Chapter XIII

Daryl and Mark

". . . oh, my God, these kids are really pumped up.
They had these kids thinking there wasn't anything
they couldn't become."

This is the story of Daryl and Mark. It may read like a fairy tale. But it is not fiction.

The story begins when Philadelphia investors Mark Solomon and Peter S. Miller attended their first meeting as members of the Gesu board of trustees. The children, carefully rehearsed, welcomed the guests and showed them around. One of the children, 13-year-old Daryl Shore, was tall and lanky, which led Miller to ask him if he liked basketball. Daryl did. Miller mentioned that he had tickets to 76ers games and would Daryl like to go. Daryl said he certainly would.

Apparently Miller didn't respond fast enough. A few days later Daryl dug through the telephone book, found the number for CMS, Solomon and Miller's investment company, and called their office. When he got Miller on the phone, he said, I met you last week, you promised to take me to a Sixers game, and I haven't heard from you.

After they attended a game, Daryl began visiting the CMS offices regularly, observing, running errands, and Solomon discovered how difficult Daryl's living circumstances were. Solomon, who was at the time not married, took him fishing, took him to Martha's Vineyard and to the best restaurants in Philadelphia, "things I take for granted now," Daryl said not long ago.

This was as far as imaginable from Daryl's earlier life. His father, a truck driver who was in and out of work, enrolled him at Gesu in the 3rd grade because he wanted Daryl to receive a good education. His mother, who had earned a degree from North Carolina Agricultural and Technical University, was a recovering alcoholic, clean and functional for fourteen years before relapsing during Daryl's childhood.

In the 4th and 5th grades, during which he was shuttled among his grandmother, aunts, and family friends, he tested the patience of Sister Ellen and Father Neil, cursing, flipping desks. For the next three years he lived with his father's sister in North

Philadelphia, within walking distance of school, and his teachers began to get a handle on him.

The turning point came while he was in the 7th grade. Daryl's family could not afford tuition, but he had heard all along that the school would waive his fees. Then he received in the mail a note stating that if tuition was not paid he would have to leave—in his mind a betrayal by the school. The next day, called to Sister Ellen's office, Daryl worried that he had done something wrong. The tuition bill was a mistaken form notice, she told him; don't worry about it. She had called him in, rather, to let him know that he had scored the highest mark in the entire school on an intelligence test.

That evening, Daryl was busily studying at his grandmother's home when she walked in. What are you doing? I'm studying. A few minutes later, he found his grandmother sitting quietly, her eyes closed. What are you doing? She was thanking God.

By the 8th grade, grasping the importance of academic achievement and influenced by his exposure to Solomon's sophisticated world, Daryl saw his life taking a different shape. When a reporter for a Philadelphia Catholic newspaper visited Gesu, he asked Daryl what he wanted to be when he grew up. "An entrepreneur," Daryl replied. "Do you know how to spell 'entrepreneur'?" the skeptical reporter asked. "No," Daryl told him, "but I know how to spell CEO."

Upon graduation from Gesu he attended, thanks to Solomon and other supporters, the private Westtown School, an academy founded by Quakers in Westtown, Pennsylvania near Philadelphia. One day at Solomon's house, Daryl borrowed a sweatshirt with the lettering "Emory," the university in Atlanta that Mark's son attended. Although he planned to attend college in New England, he researched Emory, found that it had a good record with African-Americans, played non-scholarship Division III sports, and wasn't too small or too large.

Daryl, who has grown to six feet, six inches tall, graduated in the class of 2003 at Emory, where he double majored in economics and political science. His primary disappointment there was cracked vertebrae, leading to back surgery and the end of any inter-collegiate basketball hopes. He thinks he might settle in Atlanta, the capital of the Southeast, where he volunteered with Big Brothers/Big Sisters and as a United Way intern.

But for now he is in Washington, where his investment experience and considerable presence overcame spirited competition to earn him a post as a business analyst at Fannie Mae. He expects to pursue an MBA and eventually to work with private equity investments, as Solomon does.

Daryl is the first graduate everyone at Gesu mentions. "I realize I'm the poster boy," he said with a smile. "That's fine. Gesu is my family. It has my undying love." When his biological father died the week before he went to college, Father Neil delivered the eulogy.

But he has another family now, Mark Solomon's family, with whom Daryl has lived since he was fourteen. "I've taken care of him,' Solomon said. "I've treated him like my son ever since. My house is his house." For his part, Daryl said, "I have an unconditional commitment to Mark."

*   *   *

Shortly before Thanksgiving in 1973, Mark Solomon received a telephone call from one of his partners, Bob Spivak. Spivak said he had always wanted to go to Israel, had never been there, and was leaving on Saturday, two days later. "I decided that life is a matter of sharing experience with people you really like," Spivak told Solomon, "so as much as I want to go, I'm not going unless you go with me."

Solomon, naturally, replied that he was too busy. To which Spivak said, "Listen, I know you're busy, I know you've got a lot of things going on. But if you stay home, five years from today, you won't be able to tell me what you did with these four days. If on the other hand we go to Israel together, it's something we'll remember together and share, not just for five years but for the rest of our lives. I really want you to do this."

What was the problem with our going, Carole Solomon wondered when he told his wife about the invitation; after all, neither of them had been to Israel. "It changed my life," Mark said. Hers, too. Carole (no longer married to Mark) is a Jewish woman who grew up in Philadelphia with Christmas trees and Easter egg hunts. The trip to Israel inspired her to take an active role in Jewish philanthropy; she later became the first woman ever to serve as national chairperson of the United Jewish Appeal.

The trip they took was organized by Philadelphia Jewish leaders to assess Israel's needs shortly after the Yom Kippur war. The group first visited an absorption center, an Israeli creation where newcomers are introduced to the nation and helped to find homes and jobs, in general to settle in, and the impact on Mark was almost instantaneous. "We saw these kids, about 5 years old, walking down the street, holding hands, singing in Hebrew. There was nothing about them in common. One had red hair, one was blond, one looked almost like an Eskimo, kids who were black, kids of all different colors.

"I was trying to figure out what these kids had in common. It dawned on me that the one thing they had in common was that their parents, for whatever reason, were uncomfortable living in whatever country it was—Ethiopia, or Russia, or Argentina, it didn't really matter—they weren't really comfortable living as Jews in that country so they decided to come to Israel.

"A lot of things happened on the trip, but the key thing was the absorption center, seeing for the first time that all Jews were not middle-class Americans, which I had grown up thinking Jews were. I had never met a Jew from the Soviet Union before. I'd never seen a black Jew.

"So I said to Spivak, 'You know, Bob, we tell people we're in the life insurance business. The truth of the matter is, we're in the death insurance business. This country, Israel, is life insurance. This is really important.' For the first time it really came to me why this was such an important thing. Why Israel's survival was so important."

"It changed my life" might be an understatement for Solomon. Since that casual decision in November 1973, he has made about seventy-five trips to Israel and led about thirty-five missions. Once he and Spivak chartered two 747's for 1,000 people. In Philadelphia Solomon chaired Operation Moses, the 1985 rescue of Ethiopian Jews, and co-chaired Operation Exodus, which brought Jews from Russia to Israel. Today he is chairman of the board of an orphanage, a village, really, in Israel that houses 500 children at a time, from as many as forty different countries, until they are found suitable homes.

Israel, then, is one life-changing experience for this Jewish man. The other is an elementary school operated by Catholics for African-American children in the inner-city of Philadelphia.

Solomon's devotion to Gesu is actually the culmination of decades of attention to the needs of inner-city education. In the late 1960s, while a board member of Fellowship House in North Philadelphia, he became close friends with Marcus Foster, an African-American who was principal of Simon Gratz High School. Foster moved from Philadelphia to become superintendent of schools in Oakland, California, where he set out to teach the overwhelmingly black student body that if they studied and worked hard, they could prosper in America.

One day in 1973, three young black members of the Symbionese Liberation Army—the same outlaw group that would become notorious with the kidnapping of Patty Hearst—lay in hiding outside Foster's office at dusk and assassinated him with cyanide bullets. The SLA said he was poisoning the minds of black children by telling them they could succeed within the system. Solomon was crushed: "Mark Foster had a tremendous impact on me. When he was assassinated, I somehow drifted away from the mission of working with inner-city schools."

As fate would have it, the phone call inviting him to Israel came a few months later, and Solomon's philanthropic attention was concentrated on Israel until the day in 1993 that he received another fateful call—this time from Win Churchill.

*   *   *

As I looked back on my notes for this book, one of the episodes I smiled about was the first meeting between Win Churchill and Mark Solomon to talk about the Gesu School: Two men who had achieved notable professional and financial success, who shared a warm philanthropic instinct, and who exuded enormous personal charm. It would have been fun to have been there.

Here is Solomon's description: "Win calls me one day and says I need to come see you. He tells me about knowing this Jesuit from prep school [George Bur] and tells me about his interesting involvement in Gesu School. He says we need to raise a quarter-million dollars to keep this thing afloat, because the archdiocese is not going to continue to fund it. We really want to keep the school open because it serves an important need in North Philly. He says, we Catholics have no idea how to raise money. You Jews are the best. Of all the Jews I know, you're the best fund-raiser, so I need your help."

Not as easy as you think, Solomon cautioned. "Fund-raising is a process. It's education. It takes time, face to face, heart to heart. You must listen to people. It's a lot of work. It's not like sprinkling holy water."

I had wanted to examine with Solomon the question of how Gesu receives such strong support from non-Catholics, from Jews and Presbyterians, among others, and this seemed a good time. I posed the first question to Solomon this way: "When you talk to clients, many of whom will be Jewish, they might say, 'You raise money for the United Jewish Appeal. I want to give to the UJA. Why should I do this? Why shouldn't Catholics do this?' I assume some people say things very much like this to you."

"It's not about being Catholic, or not being Catholic, because most of those kids aren't Catholic," Solomon said. "It's about education, and the fact that public education in the inner city is not working. This clearly works.

"With Gesu it's a lot easier now than when we started. People recognize the need. There must be alternatives. It's not a matter of getting rid of public education. It's a fact that, for many of our clients, it's crucial to have competition. Competition is what's good. That's why there is support of the charter schools, of vouchers, of private schools, because they believe that the key to success for anybody in anything is that there be a competitive sense. We also tell them that it's in your enlightened self-interest to do this. We need to have communities full of employable people who can work and are competent. . . .

"The thing is, Gesu delivers a quality product in the following sense: the students tested reasonably comparable to their suburban peer group, number one. Number two, the education is delivered very inexpensively, and that appeals to clients. Third, the kids come out with a value system. You know, all the things that you and I, we all take for granted, that you are imbued with by your parents or grandparents growing up, many times these kids don't have.

"So it's not about religion at all. It just so happens that Catholics decided that this is their mission. Catholics are effective in urban places. You get volume. They do a helluva job. So it didn't matter whether it was Jesuit or Catholic based. It was because they were delivering on these scores. It's that simple."

Solomon's organization, CMS, began as a life-insurance company, but now it primarily pools funds from clients and partners to invest in alternatives to the stock and bond markets, illiquid investments, such as real estate and hedge funds. CMS clients are obviously "high net-worth" individuals, but, Solomon said with pride, they share two other characteristics. One is that they are entrepreneurs. The second distinction is that "they're all philanthropic. We don't do business with people unless they're philanthropic."

*   *   *

On that first day that Churchill and Solomon spoke of Gesu, Solomon promised Churchill that one day he would visit the school, take a look, and advise if he could be helpful. Not good enough, said Churchill. No time for "one day. You've got to come right now." So they got into Churchill's car and drove the ten minutes to Gesu, where no one had expected them or prepared for the visit.

"I knew the minute we walked in that I was hooked," said Solomon. "I was just blown away. We walked into a 4th grade classroom, and I say to the kids, 'what do you want to do when you grow up?' One kid says, 'Pediatrician.' I asked him if he knew what that is. He said, 'Yes, it's a doctor who takes care of children.' The next kid says, 'Astronaut.' I turned around to Win and said, 'Oh, my God, these kids are really pumped up.' They had these kids thinking there wasn't anything they couldn't become."

They had barely left the building when Solomon pledged his support, promising to get friends and clients involved. He would invite them to his office downtown in the morning or for lunch, then drive them to the school, encourage them to walk the halls, visit classrooms, meet the children.

"Driving back, I would say to them: Listen, if we went away for a weekend to talk about the problems of inner-city education, and brought in all kinds of resources, great people who were really experienced in this field, people like you and me who care about the subject, at the end of the weekend, what we would do is, we would invent the Gesu School.

"That would be the end result. Then we'd have to go out and raise all the money, find a building, find the people to teach, and get the kids. It would take us years. And a lot of money. This is already here. We don't have to do anything except write a check. It exists."

Not only that. If Win hadn't called, Mark would not have met Daryl.

Chapter XIV

Giving to Real Life Kids

"There's only one reason to be around Gesu, and that is concern for the kids."

The Gesu School has never been awash in money and isn't likely ever to be. After all, the very idea that a little Catholic grammar school could raise millions of dollars for the purpose of providing a first-class education for black children in North Philadelphia is a daring stretch. But Gesu has raised money, a good deal more than might have been expected a few years ago, thanks to a core of dedicated supporters and a growing number of energized friends, and those allies have every reason to believe that it will continue to find the funds to continue its mission.

The task is staggering. Gesu officially charges tuition of $1,820, yet spends $5,200 per child per year. Although this operating figure is almost laughably modest by the measure of most private and public schools, tuition payments cover only about 18% of the budget because more than 80% of the students need partial or full scholarships – 357 of 430 in the academic year 2003-4. Nearly three-quarters of these children qualify for free or reduced-cost breakfast and lunch programs.

So Gesu must raise about $1.5 million annually just to operate. It needs more funds if it is to expand to serve more children and more families in the North Philadelphia neighborhood. This will never be easy. And it can never stop.

The task began even before the school became independent, before the parish was suppressed, when the Jesuit province of Maryland, the archdiocese of Philadelphia, and the straitened parishioners of Gesu provided its support. As the size of the congregation dwindled through the 1970s and '80s, the parish council settled on its fundamental priority: saving the school. At that time the school occupied only the second floor of its current building. The first floor was rented to other organizations, and the third floor, as well as half the basement, was deserted and in disrepair.

Clearly the building needed significant renovation. The pastor, William Perkins, worked with the Jesuit provincial,

James Devereux, to secure a $1 million contribution from the Maryland province to adapt the structure to new uses. Part of the first floor was to become a mini-worship-center for the Gesu congregation, so that the historic church—far larger than the congregation needed and far more expensive to maintain than it could afford—could be shuttered except for special occasions.

In 1988 Father Perkins left the Society of Jesus, and George Bur, who had been assistant pastor since 1985, took charge. About the same time a nearby Catholic school closed, leaving Gesu to absorb its children and begin an expansion from a 175-student school to the more than 400 of today. The increased enrollment required, however, that much of the first floor be converted to school use as well.

It was about then that Win Churchill made his fateful visit to Gesu. Bur was already working to raise supplementary funds, but he had other problems and, as he is first to observe, fund-raising is not his forte. Churchill, on the other hand, knows how to put together packages of money, and he saw a niche in which he might help his former Prep schoolmate and this struggling school. In 1988 he contributed $50,000 to fund a development effort independent of the longtime support groups. Shortly afterward Churchill began to assemble a Gesu Development Board and cultivate donor relationships.

This led to the first long-term financial effort, called the Sponsorship Campaign, which lasted from 1991 to 1993 (the year of suppression). Less a "campaign" than a "strategy," it was designed mainly to attract tuition sponsors for individual students, donors willing to commit $2,400 per year, a plan the school continues today with good success. That first drive raised about $275,000, $110,000 of which came from the Jesuit province. A relatively modest beginning, but a beginning, nonetheless.

With the suppression of the parish in 1993, and agreement that the archdiocese would offer a decreasing sum over the next five years, fund-raising became, as one supporter put it, "a do-or-die proposition."

What followed was called officially the Millennium Campaign, led by Mark Solomon and his CMS colleague Peter Miller. Inaugurated in the autumn of 1993, Millennium set a goal of $1.5 million for operating expenses in five-year pledges, and by May 1996 pledges had topped $1.7 million. This success provided a measure of stability that enabled the school's leadership to begin thinking beyond survival toward ambition—adding programs, bettering teacher pay, strengthening financial aid.

As the school continued to prove to everyone, old friends and new alike, how valuable it was, the ambitions of its supporters grew. Another financial campaign, called Children Succeeding, was launched in autumn 1997, chaired by Ralph Saul, the retired chief executive of the insurance giant CIGNA. Its stated goal was $3 million; in little more than two years, it had gained $4.1 million in gifts and pledges.

The Children Succeeding drive planted another milestone: an organized endowment for the school, which had been a goal of its benefactors for some time. They knew that Gesu was not going to build an endowment in the tens or hundreds of millions like many colleges, but they also knew that it was risky to rely on regular solicitation for all operating expenses. An endowment throwing off 5% or more annually could give the school a financial base.

Thus $500,000 of the Children Succeeding campaign was earmarked for endowment. That total included a $200,000 challenge grant from trustee Peter Gould and a $120,000 gift from the William Simon Foundation that stipulated 15% for endowment. As the campaign rolled well past its goal, the trustees decided to commit $200,000 beyond the earmark. So an endowment that was essentially zero as late as 1999 had risen to about $700,000 by summer 2000.

Now came Churchill with what Kevin Smith-Fagan, then Gesu's director of development, called "astonishing news." Win would contribute $1 million to the endowment; his gift would be a challenge, seeking four other $1 million donors so that Gesu could add a total of $5 million to its endowment (not that anyone thought Churchill would withdraw his gift if the challenge were not met).

Soon four contributors met the Churchill challenge: Mr. and Mrs. James Kim; he is chairman of the semi-conductor company Amkor Technology and a friend of Churchill, who sits on the Amkor board. Mr. and Mrs. John J. F. Sherrerd, "Jay" to his many friends, a Main Line investment manager and Gesu trustee. The Hubbard Family Foundation, through Dr. Anne Hubbard, a radiologist at Children's Hospital of Pennsylvania and a Gesu trustee. Mr. and Mrs. H. F. (Gerry) Lenfest, he the cable-television industry pioneer whose company merged into Comcast.

The Lenfest support has become a family affair. For the wedding of their son Chase, the invitations asked that guests not send the couple gifts and suggested contributions to Gesu and the Police Athletic League.

With this infusion, the endowment rose by spring 2003 to $4.2 million (plus the completion of confirmed pledges from the challenge), despite difficult investment conditions. It was projected to nearly $5 million in the next fiscal year, and endowment income is becoming a significant element of the school's annual budget. Smith-Fagan hoped for an endowment of $15 million, which he termed "a distant ideal," perhaps seven years.

Gesu also organized its first formal Annual Fund drive in 1999-2000, producing $362,000. Sherrerd's experience as a longtime trustee for Princeton University taught him the importance of an annual fund, not only for the dollars it produces but also for the continuing loyalty it engenders among a school's friends. The Gesu Annual Fund, led by Sherrerd, jumped by 55% in its second year to a total of $564,000; by the 2002-03 fiscal year it passed a goal of $610,000, and the next year scheduled an aggressive goal of $710,000.

"The most amazing thing to me about the fund-raising success of Gesu is the word-of-mouth, the person-to-person connections," said Smith-Fagan. "It seems as if everybody has an interesting story for how they ended up getting engaged and wanting to be more involved. . . .

"Certainly there are Catholics, myself included, who have a primary motivation for living out their faith, with a sense of ministry at Gesu. There are folks, Ralph Saul is probably one, who are attracted because its success stands out so clearly against the landscape of failed educational efforts in North Philadelphia. Ralph looks at Gesu and says, you know, it works. . . .

"Then there are people who do look at it purely from an economic standpoint. If you sit down and say, 95% of Gesu's graduating 8th graders are going to become high-school grads on time, statistically that will double their income versus being a dropout. It's good economics to educate kids in a neighborhood where the majority of them are not going to become high-school grads, which leaves them open to much higher incidences of lawbreaking, violence, social ills. . . .

"Many people, though, just have an emotional pull. I think Jay Sherrerd is a guy who will actually look at the face of a child. I think Chris and Leif Beck are like that—they look at it on a very personal level, getting to meet, know, and appreciate the actual real-life kids. It's not sort of a theoretical or statistical donation. It's real personal."

Smith-Fagan is an example of Catholic faith and altruism in action. After working in a New York advertising agency—"I liked the job fine, but it had no soul"—he moved to Philadelphia where he shared an apartment with his sister and found a job in the development office of the Greater Philadelphia Food Bank, a hunger-relief organization in North Philly. While there he met his future wife, Nancy Smith, a Californian who had come to Philadelphia after college to work with a St. Joseph's University program that engaged undergraduates in Jesuit social-justice efforts. (She persuaded him to hyphenate his birth name, Fagan, with hers, Smith. It wasn't easy; clerks at the social-security office told him only women could do that. When he protested that this might be a violation of equal-protection laws, they decided that he could fill out the same form as women did and hyphenate his name.)

Looking for a new opportunity after eight years at the food bank, Smith-Fagan tried something very different, the development office at the elite Episcopal Academy on the Main Line. "I really learned how to raise money there," he said. One of his favorite volunteers at Episcopal was a woman whose three sons had all attended the school, Chris Beck. She didn't need to introduce him to Gesu—Nancy had belonged to the Gesu parish—but here was an enthusiastic Gesu booster from another world. Then he met Roger Van Allen, an Episcopal alumnus who was the development officer for Gesu and talked enthusiastically about it. "I thought, darn, his job sounds more interesting than my job," Smith-Fagan said. When soon afterward Van Allen told Smith-Fagan he was leaving, Smith-Fagan immediately applied, interviewed with Father Bur, and soon had the job.

I had several long conversations with Smith-Fagan last year, before he and his wife moved to her native California where he accepted a development position at a Jesuit high school in Sacramento. "I was happy at Episcopal, but it did not have the appeal to my value system, really to my soul, that Gesu did," Smith-Fagan said then. "This is just an oasis, this wonderful school for kids, kids who really need the help. North

Philadelphia doesn't have many educational opportunities. Only 4% of the people in this zip code have college degrees. With kids at Gesu coming from a neighborhood like this, and going to college at better than a 50% clip, it's pretty easy to see that you're getting something important done here. . . .

"But tuition is so artificially low, there's this yawning gap between what you can charge the families and what you need to survive. If you don't have a corporate or institutional fund-raiser behind you, like the archdiocese or a school district, the money's got to come from someplace else. Fund-raising is a very critical mix to the school surviving.

"I feel there's some sense of urgency of mission to what we do at Gesu that an elite prep school just couldn't have. Fund-raising at a place like Episcopal, parents and alumni both by and large, you're giving back to your institution. If you're a parent, you're investing in your child's education at the school. If you're an alumnus, you're giving back from a feeling of loyalty.

"Whereas at Gesu people really give for altruistic reasons. We don't offer the same kind of panache or societal standing that you might derive from taking leadership in the opera or art museum. There's only one reason to be around Gesu, and that is concern for the kids. It really is focused on the kids, an acute need that everybody can understand. And it does work. You look at the outcomes of the kids in high school, successes in going on to college, and life outcomes, and say, yes, this makes a big difference in the kids' lives."

Smith-Fagan's successor as director of development is Suzette Baird, who had held the same position for a decade at the Presbyterian Children's Village Foundation, a multi-service child-welfare and behavioral-health agency near Philadelphia. At the Village, she directed a capital campaign and supervised a 125th anniversary celebration. A graduate of the Newton College of the Sacred Heart (now part of Boston College), and holder of a master's degree in political science from Notre Dame, Baird has held a variety of public relations and development jobs in Chicago and Philadelphia.

Chris Beck, an experienced fund-raiser herself, is "extremely pleased" with Baird's experience and her "enthusiastic commitment" to Gesu. "This is a very special place," Baird said. From a development perspective, she sees the school emerging from its "formative phase," which requires her to "maintain its high-energy commitment " and broaden the base of support.

Despite the difficulties of its task, Gesu's development office, like everything else at the school, works with a short staff and short budget. One staffer maintains the data and keeps the office functioning. The associate director of development is Molly de Aguiar, a skilled young writer who, on a part-time basis, both writes and designs most of the school's printed material, including its newsletter, as well as helping organize special events. Also an experienced fund-raiser—and someone dedicated to what Gesu represents—de Aguiar worked in the development office of Philadelphia's stellar performing arts facility, now known as the Kimmel Center, before joining the school.

One of the development office's most difficult tasks is to connect with Gesu graduates, which is a lot harder than one might think. These children become "alumni" at about the age of fourteen, after which they go on to different high schools, many to colleges, then to careers. They and their families move frequently, far more than average, both around Philadelphia and elsewhere; their family connections also can be hard to follow, since many are raised by a single parent, who may remarry, or by grandparents or other relatives.

Smith-Fagan said he is "amazed at what we don't know about our own alumni." Only accidentally did the school learn about a graduate who had acted on the hugely popular Bill

Cosby television show in the 1980s. "When you don't have a parish, you even lose the social center of the families who are geographically close," he said.

Connecting with alumni can benefit the school in a number of ways. It can attract volunteers for all manner of projects and mentors for current students. It can spotlight for today's children adult role models, living examples of the positive things that await those who pursue a meaningful education. And over the years it can produce new leaders, a second generation capable of taking hold from supporters who nursed the school through its independent infancy.

Admittedly, Smith-Fagan knew, Gesu alumni do not yet form a pool of major financial prospects. "So in their stead are people who somehow end up involved in this little corner of North Philadelphia. People's paths here vary, but the punch line is always the same: 'When I walked in, I fell in love with the place.'"

Chapter XV

A Commitment to the Inner City

". . . we thought, this has got to be one of the best things we could do."

Win Churchill likes to say that with the exception of the Philadelphia Museum of Art and the Philadelphia Orchestra, the Gesu School has the most elite board of trustees of any eleemosynary institution in the city. How can this be so?

One of those trustees (and the new president), Chris Beck, has an immediate answer: "The inner city." The Gesu board is united by a belief that what occurs in the urban core is important—not merely to the people who live there, but also to the entire city, and its environs as well—and vitally important is the need to educate the youngsters of the inner city to help them achieve more fulfilling lives and to be competent workers and productive citizens.

This dedication, of course, reaches beyond the board of trustees, to the hundreds by now of women and men who have contributed their resources, financial, mental, and physical.

Gesu is a glory because of the efforts of too many people to name in a single volume. It is Father Bur and Sister Ellen and Win Churchill, who are noted at some length here. It is the teachers, for whom the phrase overworked and underpaid is not a cliché but a simple truth. It is the students, whose bright faces demonstrate their eagerness to learn, and the parents, who understand what this place means to their children, their families, now and into the future. Gesu is critical to their very lives; without it many might slip into the dregs of society.

There is another group of people who could if they chose ignore Gesu. As a group they are highly educated, professionally successful, financially secure. Some of them live within the city limits of Philadelphia, but most live in neighboring towns, especially along what might be recognized as the most famous string of suburbs in the nation, known as the Main Line. These are brief stories about a few of them.

*   *   *

Like so many others, John J. F. Sherrerd, "Jay" to his friends, wasn't solicited for a contribution to Gesu, just invited to visit. The first visit—"They looked like such happy kids"— made a firm impression on him, and now, "Every time I go there I have such a positive feeling about the school."

Yet when Sherrerd joined the board, he was startled to learn that Gesu was mainly asking for *ad hoc* gifts to cover operating expenses. A longtime trustee of Princeton University and an active fund-raiser for his alma mater, he had learned that regularized giving developed in supporters "a personal relationship" with a school that not only led them to continue every year but also encouraged them to consider major contributions.

"I did not have to be involved with Gesu for more than two or three years before becoming very enthusiastic about what they were doing and wanting to be helpful," Sherrerd said. So he led the organization of the school's first Annual Fund in 1999-2000; it produced $362,000. With Sherrerd continuing as chairman, the fund jumped by 55% the next year to a total of $564,000, and now it collects well over $600,000 every year.

Sherrerd preaches the value of organized, long-term contributions. He and his friend, neighbor, and business partner, A. Morris Williams (Morris and Ruth Williams are also notable Gesu donors) have developed a philosophy designed to maintain "balance" in their philanthropy. On one side are what Sherrerd called cultural charities such as museums, music, and zoos. On the other are more individually targeted gifts, helping people in need, the most obvious outlet being the United Way. Schools and colleges, significant beneficiaries from both of their families, come in between.

Although Sherrerd was a regular donor to Gesu, when Win Churchill issued the million-dollar challenge he understood there was more to be done. "I thought, look, I can afford the million dollars relative to a lot of other things my wife and I might like to do with our money," Sherrerd said. "She and I support other things, Princeton, Smith College which she attended, the art museum, but we thought, this has got to be one of the best things we could do."

Now that Gesu has an endowment anchored by the million-dollar gifts, Sherrerd leads an investment committee that oversees the growing funds. The time will come, he believes, when endowment will throw off income critical to the school's operations, not tens of millions like Princeton's but a worthy sum nonetheless.

*   *   *

Like a lot of others, Lenny Klehr learned about the Gesu School through Win Churchill and Mark Solomon. It was on a trip to Israel organized by Solomon that Klehr met Churchill: "We hit it off and became friends and started doing work together," legal matters and business deals. The next step was straightforward, Klehr said: "In civic involvement, people tend to turn to those people that they value and they associate with. Win had decided that Gesu was going to be the main focus of his [involvement], and he asked a bunch of friends to help out.

"The thing that attracted me to Gesu was the ability of the staff, led by George and Sister Ellen, to get such positive results with kids," said Klehr. "For many generations in urban education, the failures are legion. Here were very dedicated people who were on a mission, who were successful by anyone's standards in educating and bringing about the successful development of kids who under other circumstances, if they hadn't attended the Gesu School, wouldn't have had that success. . . . I just think it's a great thing to be part of."

He and his wife Susan are, moreover, believers in the city and committed to the education of its young people. The Klehrs have lived for nearly twenty years in the Fairmont area, largely gentrified now, but almost as close to the struggling Gesu neighborhood as it is to his Center City office. He is on the board of another independent school in the city; she, a native Philadelphian, is a trustee of Franklin & Marshall College, where they met as undergraduates. Together they started a tutoring program for neighborhood children at their synagogue in the Spring Garden neighborhood, something of a "faith-based initiative" that meets four days a week.

Klehr, who grew up near Newark, New Jersey, attended Temple Law School and has practiced ever since in the city, where he is not only a lawyer of repute but also a political player of consequence. Klehr was a law school classmate of Philadelphia Mayor John Street, was a law partner of Street's, was chairman of his finance committee during a four-way primary and a hard-fought general election campaign, and chaired his transition committee.

"What's the significance [of what Gesu is doing]? At one level, I don't view this as socially significant. I view the Gesu School as a place that has a great impact on the students who are there, and their families, and that really on an everyday basis is what's important: that these 400 kids every year get a solid education, stay in school, and graduate from high school. Gesu may not be producing physicists for Harvard. But these are kids who are coming from an area where there's 60 to 70% high-school dropout rates. These people face a very difficult life in our society. The Gesu School is giving kids the foundation and development skills to go and successfully complete high school and move on beyond that. . . . their families' first generations of teachers and professionals and office workers. I think that's important.

"To me, the social significance, though, from a political point of view, is that there's a general feeling in the General Assembly in Harrisburg [the state capital where funding is decided] that certain minorities are not educable, and no matter how much money you pump into something, the system is so broken and so beyond repair that it makes no difference.

"What the Gesu shows is that under certain very specific kinds of facts and circumstances, the education is flourishing. Can we repeat it again tomorrow? No, you can't repeat the Gesu School a thousand times, because there's aren't a thousand Father Georges and Sister Ellens and their crew that do it for children because they're on God's mission. You've got to have different ways to replicate it in a public system. But it shows, it demonstrates, a larger political thing—that it can be done. It can be done with enough thinking about it, and hard work, and effort, and commitment."

*　　　*　　　*

Ralph Saul met Gordon Cooney when both worked at the Securities and Exchange Commission in the late 1950s, and when Saul moved to Philadelphia in 1974 to lead the Insurance Company of North America, the Saul and Cooney families established a close friendship. Saul, a lawyer, eventually helped guide INA into its merger with Connecticut General and became co-chief executive of the combined company, CIGNA, then chairman of its board before his retirement. It was in the early 1990s that Patricia Cooney, who knew of Saul's serious concerns about education and was certain that he would be attracted by Gesu, arranged for him to meet Father Bur and Win Churchill.

Saul was intrigued by what they told him, and, like so many others, was instantly hooked. "The first time I saw the school, I thought, well, it's wonderful. The atmosphere was so nurturing and supporting." Before long Saul had agreed to join the board of trustees, but his deeds go much further. He chaired the school's

Children Succeeding campaign, which began in 1997 with a goal of $3 million and closed two years later with gifts and pledges totaling more than $4.1 million. The campaign was significant to Gesu's future also because it established the school's first endowment.

Saul is, of course, an important financial contributor himself, but more, a pivotal figure who has introduced the school to any number of supporters, financial and otherwise. He thinks his "major contribution" is connecting the school with John DiIulio. They met when DiIulio, a native Philadelphian, was a visiting scholar at the Brookings Institution in Washington, where Saul, a loyal adopted Philadelphian, was a trustee. "I saw that he was a man of action," Saul said. "He writes scholarly and policy papers, but he doesn't just sit around; he wants to join that with a life of action."

When DiIulio returned to Philadelphia, Saul arranged lunch for him with Churchill and Bur, which led to his joining the board and helping bring "a major transformation to the institution." DiIulio, in turn, urged William J. Bennett, the former Secretary of Education, and Tim Russert, the Washington bureau chief of NBC News, to join the board and brought them and others together for a seminar at Gesu on what came to be known as "faith-based education." "I'll never forget his phrase," Saul said about DiIulio: "He said, 'This is going to make Gesu the poster child of faith-based education.' And he was quite right." The seminar, conceived as a one-shot event, has proven so successful that it is convened with a different but related theme every year.

Saul's recruiting zeal knows essentially no bounds. He once asked a driver on the way to the airport if he knew "any rich Catholic ladies." The driver did, and she now contributes $5,000 a year. Primarily though, Saul has helped bring other leading Philadelphians to the board. "We have a very good, solid base of business people, and that's absolutely essential," he said, "but we also have a strong community base, representatives of the church and education."

As a businessman, Saul is cognizant that schools like Gesu will always need money, "but it's essential they have a soul. If they don't have a soul, what's the point. Father Bur and Sister Ellen have given Gesu a soul."

*   *   *

James Kim was born under the Japanese occupation of Korea, and even after World War II ended, and even in a family that would be called "middle class," life was a struggle. "I went through all kinds of things, the Korean War, starvation," Kim said. "Today Korea is rich, but in those years even the middle class didn't really have enough to support their children."

One way to vault ahead, Kim and his businessman/politician father decided, was to pursue an American education, which Jim did at the University of Pennsylvania's Wharton School; his economics degree led him to a teaching position at Villanova University on Philadelphia's Main Line. He might have spent his career on a university faculty—"my wife says that was the best time of her life; I was home regularly"—if his elderly father's business, manufacturing semi-conductors, had not run into financial trouble in the late 1960s.

Kim said he didn't understand semi-conductors, but he knew how to find engineers who did: "And I learned it. That's how I got involved." Over three decades he built a multinational technology group—the parent is Amkor Technology—that employs more than 10,000 people in South Korea, the Philippines, and the United States. "I'm a creator," Kim said proudly. "I'm not a consumer. I've always created something, created jobs for people."

It is no surprise that he met Win Churchill through business contacts and asked him to join the Amkor board of directors. It is also no surprise that Churchill "kind of opened the door for me to look at Gesu," said Kim, "and I was glad to support it because it is a great cause."

Gesu combines two special opportunities for Kim—inner-city social problems and education. Having already endowed a chair in health economics at the Wharton School, he took a similar giant step in becoming one of the four million-dollar donors who met the Churchill challenge for Gesu. "Those inner-city children are in a vicious cycle; when you are poor you cannot get out. So the question is how are you going to come out. If one child is taken out of there, and into the mainstream to get an education, he will not go back to that cycle again, hopefully. I think that is a very tedious way of doing it, not a massive way, but you have some influence on someone's life."

Although he remains active in his businesses, Kim is looking for other ways "to give back" socially, helping Korean students in the United States for one. "Some people think there is a timetable, that you have to do everything in your lifetime. But we've had 2000 years of problems, and we can't solve them all in a lifetime. Therefore what you do is just contribute a little bit."

*   *   *

Given Gesu's modest budget, and over-scheduled teaching and administrative staff, the school counts heavily on a corps of volunteers that over the years has numbered in the hundreds. They assist teachers and tutor children, cook lunches and answer telephones, sweep up and paint the building.

John Thomas, educated in the Philadelphia parochial school system, was chief counsel in the FBI's Philadelphia office for more than two decades before retiring. Now he spends three full days a week working with 4th through 8th grade students who need "a little extra help" with mathematics. Many other tutors are retired school teachers who come from all over the area to help with various curricular needs, working with young readers on a particular goal.

Gesu benefits from communal efforts by organizations whose ties to the school are historic, for example, Old St. Joseph's, the original Jesuit parish on Society Hill in Center City. One Old St. Joe's parishioner, Jack McGrath, enjoyed his time so much with the summer program that he asked Sister Ellen if she could find something for him to do during the academic year. A new 1st grade teacher could use some help, she suggested, and since then McGrath has worked with two other 1st grade teachers and dozens of children.

Similarly, members of the Fathers' Club at neighboring St. Joe's Prep arrive at Gesu on the second Saturday of each month, sometimes more than thirty strong, in a program that began more than a decade ago. "They paint, they clean," said Father Neil. "They built our stage in the basement, they built covers for our pipes, they plastered, they caulked. You name it, they've done it." Parents, of course, pitch in. A group of parents joined with the St. Joe's fathers to construct a Gesu playground on the roof of the Prep gym.

Leona Joseph, whose daughter is a Gesu student, ranks among the most unusual volunteers. Once a week she spends forty-five minutes teaching 2nd and 3rd grade girls the art of African drumming, which is more than cultural; it also promotes skills such as teamwork, hand-eye coordination, leadership, and self-expression. Then she spends forty-five minutes teaching them about hygiene and nutrition.

"Drumming is really an incentive," Joseph said. "The focus of my program is to teach these girls about making positive choices.

I teach them about personal health, body development, character development, and nutrition." Joseph in fact hopes to build her lessons into a free-standing, non-profit organization that will offer girls from ages 6 to 16 health education, cultural experiences, summer trips, and career exploration.

Chapter XVI

Not the Label— the Quality

". . . each person has God-given talents, let's help each person develop them; thinking of the greater good, reaching out to the less fortunate. . ."

Chris and Leif Beck had a problem, sort of. As they approached their 30th wedding anniversary in 1994, they decided that gifts or vacation trips were not good enough; they needed a warmer way to honor each other. "We were talking about, well, should we take a trip, shall we go someplace special, 30 is a round number, give each other a special gift," Chris said. "Leif said, [instead of a gift to each other] let's find a different charity, someone who really needs it, something that would really make a difference."

It was about that time that Chris visited Mark Solomon to ask him to renew his corporate table at a celebration for her longtime favorite charity, the Arthur Ashe Youth Tennis Center in Philadelphia. After agreeing, he said, "Let me tell you about my favorite charity right now" and proceeded to describe Gesu. When Chris got home, she said to Leif, "I think we might have found our charity."

A couple of days later, Solomon drove the Becks to Gesu. "As you know once you've set foot in the school, well, we were bowled over by it," Chris said, "and just without much more convincing thought it would be a wonderful place to be involved in the future."

Back at Solomon's office, they were ready to leave when "the closer"—a fund-raiser's term for the person who clinches a charitable contribution—arrived, serendipitously, in the person of Daryl Shore. Naturally Solomon had already made certain the Becks knew about him. "Daryl's the key to this," Solomon related. "He told them how Gesu had been an oasis for him, a haven for him. If it weren't for Gesu he'd probably be dead or selling drugs or in prison. I didn't really close the gift. Daryl did."

Before leaving CMS, Chris and Leif decided to walk around the block to talk things over. "We were holding hands—we always hold hands—and Mark pulled up in his car and saw us," Chris said. "'How long did you guys say you've been married?'

We told him thirty years. He said, 'If you guys still hold hands after thirty years of marriage, you are definitely the kind of people we want.'"

Solomon knew then that Gesu would receive a gift from the Becks and expected perhaps $3,000, a round multiple of thirty for their anniversary, "which would be really significant, a nice thing for someone to do who doesn't know Gesu from a hole in the wall and is committed to a bunch of other things. Quite frankly I almost fell over when I got the check from them," many multiples of $3,000.

Almost needless to say, the Becks could not resist Solomon when he asked both of them to become Gesu trustees in 1996, the first husband-and-wife team on the board. Among their many efforts, Leif co-chaired the endowment committee, and Chris was a principal organizer of the successful-beyond-expectations Gesu symposium. "She makes everything happen, she's amazing," Solomon said. "Chris Beck is one of the greatest assets the city of Philadelphia has in the world of philanthropy. Not because of the money. Because she makes things happen."

It was with that characteristic in mind that Win Churchill called Beck one day last spring to talk about finding a successor to Father Bur as president of Gesu; both of them were part of the board's informal search committee. The assumption had been that a Jesuit would take the post, and two likely candidates were approached, but now both had decided it was not a good fit. On the phone, Beck remembered, "Win said to me, would you consider [the presidency]? I just said, 'are you kidding.' I think I laughed, because, at this stage of my life, I couldn't imagine that. He said, think about it, so, OK, I'll think about it."

Actually Churchill had been thinking about it for quite awhile. "In [my] business I'm always on the lookout for managers, and I knew Chris [would fit]. Whether or not one had any experience as a school administrator is to me largely irrelevant." He said he had first broached the subject with her weeks earlier after a meeting they had attended together at St. Joseph's Prep—"floating the fly," in his fisherman's term. He recalled her laughing off the suggestion then but wasn't surprised at her later response "because I wouldn't have asked her if I hadn't thought it was a pretty good thing."

After the Churchill call Chris described the conversation to Leif, who responded at once, "That's a match made in heaven. You definitely should do this. At least think about it."

"I was kind of blown away," said Chris. "My life was pretty much on track and very comfortable. I was blown away first of all by Win's suggestion and then I was totally amazed by Leif's quick response. Whoa! I need some time to absorb this. So I took a walk for two hours, by myself on the beach [the Becks were vacationing in Florida]." Not long after the walk, she called Win to say she would consider the possibility; they agreed that she would think about it overnight, and the next day she called again to say she would be a candidate.

As the selection process continued, three lay people, all closely affiliated with the school, were finally considered and interviewed by the committee (which no longer included Chris). The committee agreed on her and took its nomination to the board of trustees, where the result was by no means automatic. No one questioned Beck's ability as a leader, and no one questioned her dedication to Gesu. No one expressed difficulty with a woman or even a lay person as president. Yet the problems were obvious.

Chris Beck was not African-American. She was not even Catholic. She was a white woman Presbyterian suburbanite in line to lead an independent Catholic elementary school in the inner city with all African-American students.

Father Bur took some preliminary soundings with the archdiocese of Philadelphia and found discomfort. The archdiocese no longer supported Gesu financially, but connections remained, largely through curriculum, and Sister Ellen regularly attended its principals' meetings. Officials at the archdiocese did not approve of placing a non-Catholic in charge.

The board meeting May 16, 2002, was lively, a clear demonstration of how seriously the trustees took their responsibility, both in relation to the Beck nomination and to the school's future generally. Most of the comments began with a preamble—Chris Beck's leadership skills and her deep religious faith are unquestioned. Still, some trustees raised the issue of maintaining Gesu's values and certainly communicating to its constituencies that its mission had not changed. Others wondered how the neighborhood and the parents would react to the choice of a woman who was neither Catholic nor African-American. It was crucial, said an African-American woman trustee, that the selection be communicated correctly to the public, recalling that many had been hurt in the past by cursory explanations.

Two trustees who had been considered presidential possibilities, Ed Beckett, himself a former Jesuit, and Byron McCook, the last leader of the Gesu Parish Council, expressed strong support for Beck. So did Churchill and Father Bur, who also noted that both the Jesuit Maryland province and the Immaculate Heart order were reiterating their commitment to Gesu.

For Churchill this was "one of the best board meetings ever. It was a great discussion. As the discussion played out, there couldn't have been a better way to ratify the selection." He felt the board members exploring broadly the kind of person they needed, someone with a sympathetic understanding of the circumstances. For instance, he observed with a smile, "Gandhi would have a sympathetic understanding, and he never saw North Philadelphia."

"Ultimately, what you're trying to get at is, who is this person?" Churchill said. "We have shorthand ways. A Jesuit—that's shorthand for certain characteristics that we hope are going to be there. Or you have female, certain characteristics. It's not the tag that you want, it's the characteristics.

"What you're really trying to get at is the qualities of the person, not some labels. That's what the discussion was all about. It wasn't about Chris at all. It was really about trying to arrive at the fact that this was a wise choice, a wise recommendation on the part of the search committee." After an hour and a half of discussion, Chris Beck was invited into the meeting room to a standing ovation.

She knows, though, that difficult challenges lie ahead. "How do you follow a Jesuit priest," Beck asks rhetorically. That acknowledged, "We want to reassure people, we want to keep everyone's trust. Step one for me is to build everyone's confidence, the trust of [Gesu's many] constituencies." In order to maintain that trust, "one really significant aspect in the leadership transition is focusing on and continuing and finding ways to reinforce the Jesuit heritage of the school, especially with a non-Catholic leader. That's an important priority for me. And it will happen."

Before embarking on her new role, Beck counseled with Eugene Bay, the longtime senior pastor of her church, Bryn Mawr Presbyterian Church, partly to talk about difficult issues that she as a Protestant might encounter within a Catholic institution. "A pretty amazing person, quietly but deeply spiritual," Bay says of her, noting that Beck asked him to refer her to books of prayers that would help prepare her for the responsibility. "I find it remarkable," he said, "that at a time when she could be choosing a life of ease, Chris is not only willing but eager to take on this new challenge."

She is confident. "My overall feeling is one of great comfort and connection, even though I'm not a Catholic. I think the principles and the values that are espoused in the teaching of

Ignatius—each person has God-given talents, let's help each person develop them; thinking of the greater good, reaching out to the less fortunate—these are basic Christian things. I feel very comfortable with all of them."

Beck's standing in the African-American neighborhood and parental communities is likely to rise as more people learn about the arc of her life and her experiences. Christine Safford grew up in Lansdowne, suburban Philadelphia, the only child of an architect father and a homemaker-civic activist mother. At the age of ten she started playing tennis and excelled at once; she qualified for national competition in the 15-and-under girls division and at the age of 17 was ranked number twelve nationally for 18-and-unders.

That qualified Chris for the tennis experience of her life. Earning a place in the U.S. Nationals at Forest Hills, New York (the national tournament was all-amateur; professionals then made their living giving lessons at country clubs or barnstorming the country in search of exhibition opponents), she drew as her first-round opponent the defending champion Darlene Hard. Tradition called for the defending champion to play her first match in the stadium, so here was Chris, just turned 18, escorted to center court next to Hard, carrying a bouquet, standing at attention for the national anthem, then competing against a woman who was called "the last of the great amateur players." It wasn't so bad after play began. Chris won two games in each set.

Chris continued to compete while a student at Queens College in Charlotte, North Carolina and during a junior year abroad at the University of Vienna, earning a place on the junior Wightman Cup team, ranking in the top three dozen American women. Then came another life-altering Forest Hills experience. She had met Leif Beck briefly at a Philadelphia tennis tournament when she was 12 and he 21, a star tennis player at Duke

University—"I had this mad crush on him but I was a little girl."
By the summer of 1963 she had grown up, and when a friend of
Leif's asked Chris for a date during the national tournament, Leif
figured out a way to come along. By the following spring they
were engaged and in November 1964—Leif was now a lawyer in
Philadelphia—they married.

Because amateur tennis was a part-time experience for even
the best players, Chris and Leif (he had also been nationally
ranked and competed at Forest Hills) continued to play the lawn-
tennis circuit. At a tournament in North Carolina in 1968, they
learned something that changed both their lives. It concerned a
new program founded by Arthur Ashe; his UCLA teammate
Charlie Pasarell, a native Puerto Rican, and another friend,
Sheridan Snyder, a Virginian, that they would call the National
Junior Tennis League.

Chris Beck and Arthur Ashe—who later that summer would
win the first ever U.S. Open tournament—had known each
other for years. They shared a birthday—the same day, the same
year—but they grew up in sharply contrasting circumstances,
she in suburban Philadelphia, he in the black ghetto of
Richmond, Virginia. They met when both competed in a 15-
and-under tennis tournament at a country club in Wilmington,
Delaware, a telling day for Chris because she discovered that
Arthur and other black boys were not allowed to use the locker
room; in her "protected life," she had never before witnessed
blatant racial discrimination.

Over the years, Chris and Arthur became good friends, and
the message Ashe wanted to convey through the NJTL rang true
to her. [In Ashe's words] "the kids are learning life lessons,"
Beck related. "They're out there on their own; there's no time
outs, there's no coaching; they're learning self-sufficiency,
they're learning to win and lose graciously. These are lessons
that apply to whatever they're going to do in life—in school, on

the court, at the piano—everything kids do, that contributes to producing productive adults who are involved in society and making a living; productive lives and not getting into trouble."

Ashe and his friends started the first NJTL program in Harlem in 1968, and the next year Chris and Leif Beck started one in Philadelphia. They picked four playground sites in the city, tennis courts with wire nets, assembled volunteer teachers and began recruiting players (all boys then, 12-14 years old). "Leif walked the streets, sort of offering bribes," Chris said, "giving them tennis racquets and tee-shirts if they would try tennis." The tee-shirts came in bright colors, intentional contrast to the lilly-white tennis clothes that were *de rigueur* at the time. Chris and Leif worked at the Fairmont Park courts at 33rd and Diamond. It was their first experience in North Philadelphia.

"We got really involved with the kids." Chris said. "They came to our house a lot, helped decorate our Christmas trees. As our boys were born [the Becks have three sons], they came to know them." During a strike in the Philadelphia city school system, the Becks ran a tutoring program for children they had met through tennis. Two boys who were juniors in high school moved in with the Beck family for a year and a half and graduated from Upper Merion High School.

Chris led the Philadelphia youth tennis program for more than fifteen years, until she was chosen president of NJTL with about 300 chapters nationwide. During this time, she also served as Philadelphia recruiting coordinator for A Better Chance, the program that helped send inner-city students to New England prep schools and selective suburban high schools. Beck commits herself to improving education at every level. She has been a trustee for her alma mater, now Queens University of Charlotte, since 1995, an involvement she will continue, and a leader in the university's fund-raising efforts.

For Bryn Mawr Presbyterian she served on the Outreach
Council which supported missions beyond the congregation—it
spends nearly half its budget on causes outside the church
itself—and was the first woman to chair the Stewardship
Committee, the annual fund campaign. "I have little doubt that
this congregation's emphasis on outreach and mission," said
Rev. Bay, "has impacted her dedication to the Gesu School."

Bay also observed that Beck's extraordinary skill as a photog-
rapher is "one concrete way of giving expression to her spiritual
depth." She has published two books of fine-art photography,
Beyond Me, Voices of the Natural World, a collaboration with
poet Margaret Holley, and *Spirit of Summit County*, which grew
from family holiday journeys in Colorado.

Beck's last major task with junior tennis in Philadelphia has
been to chair a campaign to raise funds for a new Arthur Ashe Youth
Tennis Center, which is to be built at the western end of Fairmont
Park. It will have eight indoor courts, eight outdoor courts, a reading room and library, a fitness center, and a special education
program, all for children, most of them from the inner-city. She had
to wind that down before tackling her new task at Gesu.

Leif Beck, who left the law to build businesses in the health-
care industry, has focused his philanthropic efforts similarly,
especially religion-based health efforts for the inner city.
Through Bryn Mawr Presbyterian, Leif worked with the Diamond
Street Holistic Health Center, which is affiliated with a
Mennonite church that maintained a presence in North
Philadelphia even as much of its membership moved to the
suburbs. He also devoted energy to the Esperanza Health Center,
helping persuade doctors to move to the inner city, live near their
patients—and earn less money than they might have elsewhere—
"in the Christian tradition."

Gesu offered a somewhat different direction but a clear route.
"Gesu was so directly compelling that it was easy to join, easy to

choose," Leif said. "George Bur is that figure you like to see as a leader." Before he completed his term on the board recently, Leif served as co-chairman with Jay Sherrerd of the endowment committee, concerned both with raising and investing endowment and deciding at what level to spend it.

After Arthur Ashe died in February 1993, five months before what would have been his 50th birthday, his widow Jeanne Moutoussamy-Ashe invited the Becks to Richmond for the unveiling of his headstone July 10, a ceremony in which Maya Angelou recited her own commemorative poem. Leif asked Chris if they should accept or if she wanted to spend the big day in more celebratory fashion. She chose Richmond: "That's how I wanted to spend my 50th birthday."

On July 10, 2003, Jeanne Moutoussamy-Ashe joined the Beck family and other close friends in Villanova, Pennsylvania for a celebration of Chris's birthday.

Chapter XVII

Reflections on a New Age

"After the long centuries in the church that were the age of the bishops and then the age of the religious orders, today is the age of the laity."

The temperature outside was 99 degrees, the sun unyielding, the atmosphere sticky. Inside the historic Gesu church, the air was cool and the humanity warm. This was June 26, 2003, "A celebration in honor of George W. Bur, S.J.," marking his eighteen-year association with Gesu, the last ten as president of the independent Gesu School. Children from the school's choir sang; the matriarch of the neighborhood, Katie Robinson, led prayers; Father Bur's sibling, Sister Mary Bur, herself a high-school principal, presented gifts; and Father Bur, his colleague, Father Neil Ver'Schneider, and other Jesuits celebrated mass.

Then the congregation strolled next door to the St. Joseph's Prep, Gesu's big brother, for a dinner and tribute that assembled students and alumni, faculty, neighbors, and others among Philadelphia's leading citizens, admirers of Father Bur and devoted supporters of the Gesu School. John DiIulio, the University of Pennsylvania political scientist, moderated; the trustees chairman, Winston Churchill, the principal, Sister Ellen Convey, and Bur's successor as president, Christine Beck, paid tribute, and trustee Ralph Saul announced creation of the $250,000 "Father George Bur/Jesuit Scholarship Fund."

Sending Father Bur off to his new assignment at St. Joseph's University denoted a wrenching change for the little school. Yet nothing out of the ordinary for the Society of Jesus. As a matter of course, the provincial, or chief administrator, of the Jesuits' Maryland Province leaves his post after a six-year term and so do the rectors or superiors of Jesuit residences.

"There is from the first in our [Jesuit] history this idea that we would go wherever we would be asked to go if there was a greater need," Bur told me. "That's expressed often, even by Ignatius." I persisted, asking why Father Timothy Brown, who became the Maryland provincial in 2002, thought it necessary for Bur to leave Gesu. "I don't think he thought about that," Bur replied. "He was thinking of his needs at different places and thinking about men who are capable of doing them."

Before Father Bur was reassigned, the new provincial discussed several possibilities with him, a couple of which he did not like but a couple more that fit both his interests and abilities. One, a largely administrative position based in Baltimore, appeared a match, but Brown finally decided that Bur was needed more at St. Joseph's University.

"One of Tim's favorite words is 'reimagining,'" Bur said. "He's reimagining the province, what we can do, what we are capable of doing. The way I think about different Jesuit ministries is, we're all in this together. Tim has concern for the Gesu School, whether or not I'm there. Other Jesuits have concern for this school, and I for some other things. When we move around, we move kind of laterally, instead of up some kind of ladder."

Bur said he would not have chosen to leave, but "I'm aware that the Jesuits have been committed for a long number of years to Gesu, it's been able to flourish, and it can continue to flourish. I felt an obligation to say to the provincial, if you want me to do something else—the Society's been very generous to us here—I'm going to do something else. I didn't feel as though I should say, This is not a good time, because I think it is a good time.

"It's a wonderful job. When I described it to people who might be interested in the job, every one of them said, this is something that could really be fulfilling. But sometimes I said to them, we have such good staff, such wonderful trustees, everything's going so well, sometimes I don't do anything—everyone else is doing it. So I said to myself, it's time to give somebody else a chance at doing this job."

Apparently neither Brown nor Bur doubted at the outset that a Jesuit would be available to replace Bur at the school. "There were two Jesuits we thought could do the work," Bur said, "but neither one of them wanted to apply." Can a Jesuit be required, forced, to accept a certain position? Bur conceded that was possible, but unlikely. "There may be twisting of arms, but we would almost never do that." Instead, he observed with a smile, "Initially [Jesuits] might say no, but there is a lobbying job on them. They are cajoled."

When it became clear that cajoling wouldn't work, that a Jesuit would not replace him at the school he had led for eighteen years, Bur dug in with Chairman Churchill and the rest of the search committee to find a suitable successor. In the end he felt comfortable with all three of the final candidates, and certainly with Chris Beck; a non-Catholic laywoman, yes, but a person with strong religious beliefs.

"A person of faith" was the *sine qua non* for Father Neil, who remains at Gesu, the only Jesuit. In a conversation we had before the new president was chosen, he said: "Although it may not be crucial whether the person taking over be Jesuit or I.H.M., it is crucial that the person be a person of faith. . . . Without this dimension in the everyday decisions as well as the overall motivation in the work of the Gesu, we would rather quickly lose our focus to serve the poor, the disadvantaged, and those who are not the brightest." Having worked thirty years in the inner city, he found "those who are still working with the poor are people who have a deep personal faith that they have continued to nurture in good times and bad times, in success and failure."

When we spoke again, after Beck's selection, Father Neil said, "Certainly we have somebody who is of faith," then identified Gesu's decision as part of a broader cultural/religious change: "The only difference [with having a laywoman as president] is that one of George's roles was to keep the focus on overall Jesuit and I.H.M. charisma . . . Jesuits are learning to pass on that charism to ministries in which they are no longer very present. It is a learning process. There are a lot of things we may have taken for granted that we need to think a little more about. And that's fine."

Smoothing the transition is the fact that Bur's new posting will keep him close to Gesu. He will continue as a trustee—two other Jesuits also serve on the board, a St. Joseph's University faculty member and the pastor of Old St. Joseph's Church—and can spend time regularly at the school. He counts on developing relationships between the university and Gesu. "I would very much like to get some university students and maybe even some faculty to do research and mentoring with Gesu students." He hopes, for example, to see a longitudinal study, perhaps four or five years, beginning with 4th grade boys, focusing on why they struggle more academically than their girl classmates. He would also like to see St. Joe's students mentor some of these boys.

St. Joseph's is a happy choice not only because of its location but also for the historic connection. The university, after all, is the school built by Father Villiger and the Jesuits in North Philadelphia on land that now houses St. Joseph's Prep and Gesu. Needing more space, St. Joseph's University moved in 1927 to a campus that straddles the city line, partly in the Wynnefield section of Philadelphia and partly in Lower Merion Township of Delaware County.

Bur's presence in Philadelphia will also let him work with Beck and the board to maintain the historic relationship that Gesu has had with the Prep and even increase the cooperation as both schools reach consequential long-term decisions in such areas as facilities and curriculum. Further, "I will try to bring together energies that I know are available from our trustees, maybe Prep trustees, university trustees and staff, and possibly leaders from Old St. Joseph's Church—to bring these groups together to explore common projects," whether they be spiritual or educational.

Bur's specific assignment at St. Joseph's University is to serve as rector of the Jesuit residence. It's a complicated place. About one-third of the men are active professionals, on the faculty at St. Joseph's or working in various other assignments around the city. Roughly one-third more are retired, many from the St. Joseph's faculty. Another one-third, retired and ill, live in an infirmary at the residence. Bur will be responsible for the well-being of the community, its harmony, making certain that the men are well-suited to their work and find it satisfying, helping the provincial ascertain that the men are in the right place to do the work of the society. "I have to learn a lot about the personal lives of the men," he said.

This task is not entirely new to Bur. He just completed a six-year term as "superior" at the small residence around the corner from Gesu where he lived with eight other Jesuits, several of whom teach at the Prep. It was an assignment he could combine with the presidency of Gesu School, but the university position will clearly be more time-consuming.

Bur counts himself enthusiastic about his new assignment, but severing the direct ties to Gesu clearly occupied his mind during the early months of 2003. In an edition of the school's newsletter, he offered some "Reflections on Leaving Gesu School." Here are some excerpts:

> . . . The reaction of the children to my leaving is sometimes amusing, sometimes consoling. One boy moaned and screwed up his face, saying, "You're the only one who doesn't get after me." I suppose I am somewhat irresponsible in this regard but I rarely have the obligation of nagging kids for homework or of their discipline.
>
> The small number of eighth graders in the pre-algebra class that I teach looked gloomy when they first found out about my leaving although I reassured them that I was just "graduating" on schedule with them. . . .

Others are anxious in this time of change. Every person, in a family, for example, has a role, a place, a presence that breaks through the walls of a home and permeates its rooms. The rest of the people at Gesu will know that I am not here in the office. But new and stable, even wonderful presences will take my place.

The public should know, too, that all of the good and practical ideas of the past twelve years had their source among our chair, our staff, our principal Sister Ellen, or trustees, those who invited themselves to be our friends; these ideas resulted in the courage and resources to highlight the good that we have accomplished and to get it to grow. All those who aided in the past will continue their commitments, and I am happy to say that I will continue among the trustees.

But how do I feel personally in this time of transition? Let me mention the shame first of all so that we remember how it colors everything in North Philadelphia. There is so much wrong with the way we treat our youngest citizens in this city and we all know it. So much is left undone. So many resources that I could have mobilized but did not. Let me not overstate this but we are all affected by the sin here. Is it racism? Is it laziness? Is it our lack of hope? And we are all weakened by not naming the sin more clearly.

And I am anxious about the kids that are on the edge and that I will not continue to see each day. We hope against hope . . . but we will lose some of them. I just hope that it is not that beautiful girl who lights up the fifth grade or that second grade boy who stopped in my office to tell me that when he has a school, he's going to name it "Gesu."

Nothing other than hope motivates our families. True, sometimes they are anxious and ashamed as well. Tears of anxiety and hopelessness sometimes overcome our parents when they must discuss the future of a troublesome kid. But so much more pervasive is a spirit of hope and promise. My child will not become part of a tragic statistic. My child will be a person of whom I will be proud. And many of them pray for that more than for anything else in life. This hope is infectious. The statistics said to be typical of the neighborhood fade into the background.

When I do an inventory of my feelings, I remember the gifts that black Catholics bring to my church, gifts that the African-American bishops named as their gifts to our wider Catholic culture. Joy! A wholeness of spirit and body! A sense of community! And a spirit of forgiveness! Never do I want to separate myself from the daily reception of these gifts. Even if I find myself far away physically and short on enthusiasm, may some good spirit keep reminding me of these gifts that I received here at Gesu School.

Some of Father Bur's "reflections" he chose to leave out of the newsletter, but he expanded them upon my request. It suggests why he believes that the school will continue to be in good hands, both administratively and through its trustees; and why a new cultural and religious order appears to be at hand. Here is part of the message he added:

One trustee told us not to underestimate the negative effects of this transition. Another warned me that, while it is possible for a non-Jesuit to model the Jesuit charism, the chances of this were slim without plenty of spiritual preparation and evaluation. What can a layperson alone know about the Jesuit way of living that the Jesuits call "Our Way of Proceeding," this a phrase that is mysterious and not very inviting?

For most of my life as a Jesuit, we Jesuits in the United States continued to become a smaller and smaller group of men. Some of us ask this question, "What are we doing wrong?" Others are optimists believing that the Spirit is leading the Roman Catholic Church in a new direction. After the long centuries in the church that were the age of the bishops and then the age of the religious orders, today is the age of the laity.

For Jesuits in this part of the United States, nothing marks this new age more clearly than the recent appointment of a layperson to be president of our flagship Jesuit school, Georgetown University. At Georgetown a competent layman steeped in the traditions of the Jesuits is now the president. Some other Jesuit schools at high school and middle school levels around the country have lay presidents. This is also the future at Gesu School. In the absence of an able, willing and available Jesuit, a lay president, familiar with the traditions of the Jesuits and the I.H.M. sisters, will be the second president of the Catholic and independent Gesu School.

As a surprise gift for the farewell celebration, the staff assembled a book to which more than eighty people contributed messages and photographs. Shirley Bright, a teacher, wrote: "Children are great readers of the heart. They have read the heart of Father George Bur and they know it's a heart full of love." Mark Solomon wrote: "From the first day I met you, I knew you were doing the Lord's work on earth; for that I thank you." Father Rick Malloy, a faculty member at St. Joseph's University and a Gesu trustee, wrote: "I pray that all of us who sign 'SJ' after our name can live the life half as well as George does." Katie Robinson wrote a poem about love and concluded: "Thank you for eighteen beautiful years, for being my pastor, my brother in Christ, and my very best friend."

Chris Beck, the new president, read those tributes and added her own. She reminded the group what Father Bur had said upon the parish's closing ten years earlier: "Thanks be to God. The children give us a mission that continues to engage hundreds of volunteers and win support from outside the community."

Now, Beck continued: "Today we still say: Thanks be to God: The children give us a mission. In fact, the children are our mission. Amid so many injustices in today's society, one of the most poignant inequalities is education—the lack of quality education for each and every one of our children, regardless of race, regardless of economic consequence. I'm sure this is partly why Father Bur *had* to find a way to keep Gesu open. He had the vision and faith and commitment to save and grow this beautiful little school for the children and families of North Philadelphia.

"As I've been learning about the Jesuit philosophy of education and the teachings of Ignatius, the reasons for Gesu's success have become more and more clear. . . . George, your personification of the Jesuit ideals, your inspirational faith, and your loving commitment will guide me and all your successors at Gesu."

Chapter XVIII

Mirabile Dictu—
a School

"What this school has are these incredibly dedicated people who believe that little children are God's children, they are to be loved; and that's not necessarily the general view of society . . ."

Could it work? In 1993 the Gesu School was a pioneer, a Catholic elementary school with no parish ties, in an urban neighborhood, with mostly non-Catholic students, dependent for survival on the kindness of strangers. Yes, it could work. A decade later Gesu has survived, prospered, and looks to the future with ambition and confidence.

The 10th anniversary of this noble experiment coincided with a time of notable change. Foremost was the departure of the founding president, Father George Bur, and the selection of Christine Beck as his successor. Not to be overlooked, however, is the financial stability provided by an endowment of nearly $6 million, thanks largely to Winston Churchill's challenge, met by four other friends of the school.

The future appears bright for the Gesu School. Yet it aspires greatly, and much remains undone.

The choice of Beck to follow Father Bur tracked a momentous movement in the Catholic Church. As Bur reflected upon leaving Gesu, optimists believe that "the Spirit is leading the Roman Catholic Church in a new direction. After the long centuries in the church that were the age of the bishops and then the age of the religious orders, today is the age of the laity."

In a recent critique of two books chronicling troubles in the Catholic Church, Notre Dame historian R. Scott Appleby observed: "Countering these dismal trends is the stunning fact of postconciliar lay initiative in the church and the world. . . . [T]he laity are inheriting the mantle of institutional leadership in a vast network of Catholic universities and colleges, parochial schools, health care facilities and hospitals, and charitable and social service agencies."

Win Churchill would agree; he sees the "hand-off" from the Jesuits and I.H.M. to the laity as a critical phase in the advance of the Gesu School. In fact, he participated in a similar transition not long ago as a member of the committee seeking a new president for the Jesuits' flagship university, Georgetown in Washington, D.C. Some Georgetown trustees insisted that the president be a Jesuit, as it had always been; others like Churchill contended that it should be "the best available person" consistent with university, Jesuit, and Catholic principles. A layman was chosen. Comparing Beck's selection at Gesu, Churchill said, "It's the substance of the thing that you're after, not the form."

The ascension of the laity is a happy result of a fairer American society, Churchill believes. Catholic universities filled a crucial niche decades ago, when some institutions discriminated against Catholic students or because those students couldn't attend first-rate institutions without compromising their religious principles. "A lot of [these higher education issues] have been worked out because of the success of our society," Churchill said. "Jesuits are now realizing that there's more bang for the buck in the inner-city than maybe having suburban prep schools that send everybody to Harvard or Georgetown or Brown. So as there are fewer Jesuits, they're leavening a different loaf of bread."

Similarly, he hopes for a "refocusing" by the Jesuits of St. Joseph's Prep, from a "high-quality suburban prep school that happens to be in the inner-city" to a school "really engaged in the neighborhood, an urban prep school [that will help] people who really need it, who have much more extreme needs and many fewer choices than some other groups."

Schools like the Prep and Gesu can fill this special niche: "The Jesuit mission is really not just service to others. It's about the full realization of each individual so that he or she can then be qualified to serve others. It has nothing to do with SAT or PSAT [tests] or any of that stuff. If you define the ability to become a full person and deliver full service to others as the admission standard, then [you may or may not have lower test scores] but you're not screening for the wrong thing anymore."

That type of admission standard, Churchill believes, is one of the secrets of Gesu's broad support. He contrasts it to many other private schools, which favor family connections and thus must rely on those families and their friends for financial support. "If all people are our people, if we have that kind of mission," Churchill said, "you can raise money from all people. We recognized that from the very first day. Here you had a school that was not just taking care of 'their own people'; it was a catholic school with a small 'c.'"

Preparing the "full person" who can provide "full service" to others leads Churchill to what he considers a second hand-off—not merely to a generalized laity but also to the "natural constituency of the school"—its graduates. Daryl Shore, who is already on the board of trustees, represents the leading edge of this effort, but a growing number of stars like Maleeca Bryant, now a student at St. Peter's University, and Ronald Warren, now at the Prep, are following closely.

"Many old-line schools have their natural historic constituency, and become self-governing, self-perpetuating," Churchill said. "We [the current Gesu trustees] are a bunch of volunteers. If we are going to be successful, what will demonstrate that is gradually turning it over to its natural constituency, the graduates of the school. That's why the tracking program [for alumni], staying in touch with the kids, is important. A lot of kids who graduate will go on to wherever they go on to over the years, come back, and sit at the board table—while all of us will be playing golf in the sky. That's the rest of the job.

"We've proven, I think, with Chris, that we can do a hand-off from a Jesuit to a lay person, a lay person of a different sex and a different faith. We've proven we can abstract the qualities that are necessary to this job. We can find them readily—Chris was sitting right at our table. So if you define the qualities correctly, it's not so rare. What's rare is getting the definition of what you're looking for—what the mission is, and the qualities of the people who can fulfill this mission."

At the moment Beck is concerned with a shorter-term "generational" transition: what happens when supporters of the first decade leave the board. She has already begun smoothing that transition by persuading Susan Kim to lead the board's nominating committee. Kim is one of Gesu's younger board members; the daughter of James Kim, one of the Churchill challenge donors, and a member of the elite Philadelphia Orchestra board. "Susan is very active in the community," Beck said, "and in touch with a lot more people of her generation than Win or I would be in touch with."

Beck was herself a Gesu trustee for six years, so she knows how its board functions; further, she has served as president of both Philadelphia and national volunteer organizations. She wants to tighten the board structure, seek active committee chairmen or chairwomen, encourage committees to meet regularly, in general "get people more involved."

One case is the faculty and program committee that includes not only Sister Ellen but also a number of board members with considerable experience in education. She would like that committee to meet frequently and study special problems such as the boys' difficult academic progression. "We hope that from the vast experience of a lot of the educators maybe new ideas will surface," she said.

The most important academic effort on the table now is the inauguration of a pre-school program, two classrooms each for three and four-year-olds. "The earlier you can get the kids into a quality education, the more they can learn," Sister Ellen said. The school has accepted one class of four-year-olds since 1993, and Ellen has long campaigned for a larger pre-school, but lack of space has stymied further growth.

Instruction will be much like nursery or Head Start programs anywhere else—a lot of counting and identification of shapes and colors, an introduction to letters—things most middle-class children pick up at home but many in the Gesu demographic do not. Sister Ellen remembered one mother arriving to protest that her daughter had been reported not to know her colors; it took a meeting in the principal's office, with the four-year-old looking at pictures on the walls, to convince her otherwise.

Besides pre-school, Beck is examining other opportunities to benefit the broader Gesu family. One is to expand after-school programs, which will please working parents like Cecilia Ross-Kent, who wish the late-afternoon hours could offer "more teaching, less baby-sitting." "I think it's a huge opportunity for us to serve the children and the families," said Beck. "Right now, again, it's a space limitation. But we have the chance. It's mostly dead time for the children and we should be doing more for them."

Beck and Sister Ellen both want the after-school hours to be better used academically, programs that are difficult to fit into the regular school day. On the one hand, they can help the brightest students with honors courses, and on the other, struggling children with tutoring in subjects such as reading and public speaking. "If we can obtain more space and work out the funding, I see this as an opportunity to offer enrichment for these children," said Beck. Further, a variety of extra-curricular activities can be added: in music, for example, the school might be able to provide musical instruments and lessons for the children, and more sports can be offered beyond the twice-a-week trips to the Arthur Ashe Youth Tennis Center that a few children now take.

Gesu hopes to help its families in every way possible. Not long ago, three students and their single mother were driven from home by a winter fire, losing all their belongings. During this desperate time the school provided the only secure haven for the distraught children and has continued to ease them through the stressful experience. But the cause reaches beyond extraordinary events. "A lot of our parents are young and struggling," Beck said, "and some of them are as much at risk as the children are. We can help them learn the skills to parent a little better. They often don't have the resources, but they're working hard." To that end, two teachers have already developed a parenting class.

Another new initiative could be a literacy program for parents and grandparents who read not at all or weakly. Many children live in homes without a book, have never been read to, and naturally enough come to school with overwhelming language deficits, some of them unable to speak in sentences. "It does affect the children if the primary care-giver can't read the report card," Beck observed. "So this would be a wonderful service for everyone."

All of these efforts depend on space, which Gesu clearly needs more of. Current space is adequate for the two classrooms in each grade, but it is inadequate for all those other things, preschool or after school. A short-term answer is two rooms in the basement, which can be reconfigured and spruced up.

The longer-term prospects offer more promise. For now, though, Gesu awaits the implementation of a strategic plan developed for St. Joseph's Prep. A longtime loyal resident of North Philly, the Prep, under its new president, Father Bruce Bidinger, clearly hopes to become an even better neighbor in its neighborhood. Father Bidinger and Chris Beck have already discussed the relationship between the schools, and she is optimistic that the Prep's plans will present Gesu with opportunities for expansion.

For Churchill, it is not critical precisely how these discussions play out. "Our strategy, our long-term plan, is not a function of the type of things that are available or not available," he said. "To me, real estate is not strategy. Our strategy is, first of all, to be able to continue to do what we're doing for the long term, to protect the base. The second strategy is to do more than what you reasonably can, consistent with the strategy, to expand the financial base consonant with expansion [of the school]. . . . But it's challenging. We have had to galvanize our community here, and our supporters, and we have done it highly successfully because of the wonderful nature of the mission. . . . It's not that hard a thing to sell. But it's a recurring sales job. It has to be done every year."

Wherever or however Gesu expands, by construction or renovation, the effort will require millions of dollars. Beck is accustomed to a fund-raising challenge, that having long been one of her important voluntary activities. "Ensuring financial stability and security for the future is a huge task," she said. "I kind of sense that, because of the high visibility of the successful Churchill challenge, and because of the new big numbers, everyone sort of thinks, 'Oh, Gesu's fine, we have plenty of money.' And that's not true. Sure, three years ago we had virtually no endowment and now we're close to $6 million, and we hope that will produce $200,000 [a year]. But we project deficits in the operating budget, and we have to eliminate that.

"We have to reach out to more people, broaden our base at all levels of supporters, from those who send $10 to those who send $10,000. We need to double, triple, the endowment fund, so we don't have to raise so much money every year. Now almost $2 million a year is needed from outside the school, including the Jesuits, other gifts and grants, foundations, the archdiocese, the whole range. That's a huge challenge. We've done it successfully, and certainly we'll continue to do it successfully. But we should not be in a position of needing that much every year."

Churchill is confident about fund-raising because the school speaks for itself. "We never force the issue," he said. "We almost don't ask. I've heard it described as the Mother Theresa principle, which is just go and tell everybody what you're doing and then wait. Because we're basically looking for people who want to do this, to be a part of it. So because of the convincing nature of the mission, we've not had to go and say to somebody, 'I want $10,000.' [Instead] you do full disclosure, then you wait, patiently and in good faith, and people of good faith will be forthcoming."

How far can we carry that thought? For years now those who have watched most closely the success of Gesu have wondered: Can this success be replicated? Can a thousand little Gesus bloom? The answer is probably yes and no.

"We have discussed the possibility—really, the difficulty—of replicating the Gesu School," said trustee Leonard Klehr. "What this school has are these incredibly dedicated people who believe that little children are God's children, they are to be loved; and that's not necessarily the general view of society and everybody involved in education.

"In addition, Gesu has required massive amounts of fundraising to make a go of it. I'm not sure that can be replicated because I'm not sure there's that much energy around. The Gesu School is 400 kids, a good number, and it's exciting, and we've grown it a great deal. But the [Philadelphia] public school system has 220,000 kids. It's a much different kind of problem. I think the need is to try to make public schools great as well as to give people alternatives and choices. It's easier to make a school excellent—not easier in the sense that there's not great difficulty—but it's always easier to make it excellent on a small scale. That's been done at Gesu."

So if maintaining excellence and expanding carefully will keep its faithful busy indefinitely, Gesu does have a cousin operating only a few blocks away, the Young Scholars Charter School. (A relatively new phenomenon, charter schools are semi-independent public schools, created by private citizens who contract with a local school board or state agency; in exchange for freedom from the usual regulations, they commit to certain educational goals set out in their charter and are held accountable for student performance.) Young Scholars is different from Gesu in significant ways: it derives more than half its operating expenses from federal, state, and city funds, and, of course, must be secular, with no religious education; it is also a "middle school," with students in 6th, 7th, and 8th grades.

But there are important connections. On the Young Scholars board of trustees are several Gesu trustees, including Win Churchill, Jim Kim, Jay Sherrerd, and Mark Solomon, all of whom are among the school's largest financial contributors, and Father Bur as well. Young Scholars draws from roughly the same demographic and geographic area as Gesu, which leads to an enrollment totally African-American.

The pivot is Stanley R. Wolfe, who is director of Young Scholars and an illustration of someone who grew tired of doing well and decided to do good. A year ahead of Win Churchill at Yale Law School, Wolfe began practice at a white-shoe Philadelphia firm which he left because "I didn't like to represent thalidomide drug companies." After serving on the state environmental pollution strike force and heading the narcotics control strike force of the Pennsylvania Crime Commission, he returned to private practice and served as lead counsel on a number of class-action banking and stock manipulation cases.

Then he took early retirement from the firm at age 55, looking for some element of public service: "I wanted to spend the next ten years doing something interesting." And sure enough, here was Win Churchill. At a "thank you" party for Gesu contributors, Churchill mentioned to Wolfe a proposal for a charter school and a couple of days later, on a train to Washington, they picked up the idea. "I'd always had the idea of doing *pro bono*, and here was a chance to develop and run a project," Wolfe said. "My brother is principal of an all-minority public school in Oakland, California, so I knew it needed to be done."

Young Scholars opened with sixty 6th graders in September 1999, added 7th and 8th grades, and is inundated with applicants. Its stated mission is quite specific: academic. "We wanted to provide children in this area with the ability to go to a college-preparatory high school," said Wolfe. "We make it very clear in our literature; if you just want to play basketball, don't come here. We have a dress code, and very strict behavior standards, but academics is most important.

"I say to people, 'we're essentially a secular spin-off of Gesu.'" It's not the same school, but it represents the same ideals.

Gesu, then, is not going to franchise itself, and secular charter schools can be similar but not identical. It is the mission that can—must—be replicated. John DiIulio knows: "I'll tell you what will happen if things like the Gesu School multiply. You give me three Gesus, I'll close a medium-security prison. Give me six, I'll close two. It's the answer. From a purely civic standpoint, it's the answer."

In his vivid manner, DiIulio offers a quantitative measure of Gesu's values. Yes, he speaks figuratively, and perhaps it's too soon to identify in literal ways precisely how successful the school is. It's difficult, as we know, to track its graduates, and the school has only recently begun to try. It has no comparison studies, in part because there are so few institutions like Gesu anywhere.

Yet a body of evidence is accumulating. In a neighborhood in which only 35% of girls and boys graduate from high school, Gesu knows that more than 90% of its children do. Of the 49 students in the 8th grade graduating class of 2003, 41 went on to selective secondary schools, some private, some Catholic, some public magnet schools. For the academic year 2003-4, six boys, all of whom attended Gesu on scholarship, now attend the rigorous neighbor St. Joseph's Prep. By mid-winter 2003-4, 8th graders had received acceptances from some of Greater Philadelphia's elite secondary schools – Germantown Friends, Episcopal Academy, Penn Charter, Springside, Shipley, LaSalle, West Catholic – almost always with scholarships attached.

Each crop of new graduates seems ready to enhance their little school's reputation.

As sad as the day was a decade ago when the cardinal wiped out the Gesu parish, perhaps he did the inner-city, and its children's education, a favor. From that moment has arisen, *mirabile dictu*, a school—a school to inspire other faithful people in other places to create something similar.

They would see what the educator Gail Avicolli saw: "The whole package that you would need for a successful student is here. The opportunities are here—all the pieces are in place, the support for individual academic differences, the textbooks, the paper, the cleanliness, the health services, the counseling, the follow-through. . . . There isn't one part of their social, emotional, religious, or academic needs that is not addressed. They're providing a truly academic atmosphere for the children—it's very clear that there is a strong academic thrust—but it's very clear that this is a school that is going to treat you like family."

But what about luck? Where is it written that someone like Father Bur, someone like Sister Ellen, and someone like Win Churchill would come together at the same place and the same time, attracting and inspiring all those friends who have in turn given so much strength to this little school? Is it simply good fortune?

We leave the benediction to Sister Ellen, in a conversation I had with her about Father Bur's departure from the school:

"When I first heard the news I felt shocked, overwhelmed. But I know it will be fine. We didn't sit down one night and say, we're going to start a school. There was no blueprint for it. Something keeps guiding us. We've gone through a lot of crises and we've survived. The success of Gesu School is not based on George alone. Something bigger happened. It has to be the work of God."

A Note About Sources

The principal sources for this book are women and men who have known and cared about the Gesu School over many years and who have been instrumental in its success as an independent school. Without exception they cooperated warmly and enthusiastically in my research.

During more than two years, I formally interviewed about fifty people, a number of them several times, and Father George Bur and Sister Ellen Convey more times than I can count. All of these interviews were conducted in person, a few supplemented by telephone conversations and e-mail. All are on tape, producing more than 300 single-spaced pages of transcript. Except for rare cases when a subject asked me not to use a piece of information, the interviews were entirely on the record. Quotations in the book are not individually cited, since in nearly all cases the speaker's name accompanies the quotation or the source is apparent.

To carry out this research I made about thirty trips to Philadelphia, most to the Gesu School but also to other sites as needed. In attending meetings of trustees and social events, I was able to speak informally with dozens of people important to the school, including trustees, neighbors, parents, and children. They cannot all be named here, but they all contributed.

In addition, I read scores of news stories from newspapers in Philadelphia and elsewhere. I also benefited from websites for the Society of Jesus; the Sisters, Servants of the Immaculate Heart of Mary, and other entities. I studied a number of helpful books relating to Philadelphia, its history and its people, especially North Philadelphia and the city's Irish community. In particular, I mention two works by Dennis Clark, *The Irish in Philadelphia: Ten Generations of Urban Experience* and

Erin's Heirs: Irish Bonds of Community, and the extremely useful *Parish Boundaries: The Catholic Encounter with Race in the Twentieth-Century Urban North* by John T. McGreevy.

Most of the written material was gathered for me by Molly de Aguiar of Gesu's development staff, and also by Kevin Smith-Fagan, formerly the Chief Development Officer. They are thanked in the preface to this work, but they deserve further mention here.

All tape recordings and transcripts of interviews are in my files. All news stories used as sources are in my files. (Several of the books have been returned to the Gesu School and are available there.)

Following is more detail on the sources. (Interview subjects are identified with their title at the time of the interview, except as otherwise noted.)

PERSONAL INTERVIEWS

ADMINISTRATION OF THE GESU SCHOOL
Rev. George Bur, S.J., President (to 2003)
Christine Beck, President (beginning 2003)
Sister Ellen Convey, I.H.M., Principal
Father Neil Ver'Schneider, S.J., Chaplain
Sister Patricia McGrenra, I.H.M., Counselor
Kevin Smith-Fagan, Vice President for Development (to 2003)
Suzette Baird, Director of Development (beginning 2003)
Molly de Aguiar, Associate Director of Development

FACULTY OF THE GESU SCHOOL
(Note: Because many members of the faculty perform several duties, and because they change responsibilities over the years, their titles are not listed below. Their positions at the time of the interview are stated in the text.)

BOOKS

Byron, William J., S.J. *Jesuit Saturdays: Sharing the Ignatian Spirit with Lay Colleagues and Friends.* Chicago: Loyola Press, 2000.

The Catholic Encyclopedia, Volume XIV, 1912 - Online Edition 1999. (Article by) J. H. Pollen, transcribed by Michael Donahue

Clark, Dennis. *Erin's Heirs: Irish Bonds of Community.* Lexington: University Press of Kentucky, 1991.

Clark, Dennis. *The Irish in Philadelphia: Ten Generations of Urban Experience.* Philadelphia: Temple University Press, 1973.

Davis, Allen F., and Mark H. Haller, eds. *The Peoples of Philadelphia: A History of Ethnic Groups and Lower-Class Life, 1790-1940.* Philadelphia: Temple University Press, 1973.

Golden Jubilee, 1888-1938, Church of the Gesu, Philadelphia. (No author, editor, or publisher indicated.)

The Gesu Parish Centennial. Custombook, Inc., 1969.

Go Forth and Teach: The Characteristics of Jesuit Education. Washington, D.C.: Jesuit Secondary Education Association, 1987.

Gormley, James J., S.J. *Saint Joseph's Preparatory School: A History, 125 Years, 1851-1976.* Philadelphia: Saint Joseph's Preparatory School, 1976.

Hershberg, Theodore, ed. *Philadelphia: Work, Space, Family, and Group Experience in the 19th Century.* Oxford/New York: Oxford University Press, 1981.

McCullough, David. *John Adams.* New York: Simon & Schuster, 2001.

McGreevey, John T. *Parish Boundaries: The Catholic Encounter with Race in the Twentieth-Century Urban North.* Chicago/London: University of Chicago Press, 1996.

Ryan, John J., S.J. *Memoir of the Life of Rev. Burchard Villiger of the Society of Jesus.* Philadelphia: Press of F. McManus, Jr. & Co., 1906.

Talbot, Francis X., S.J. *Saint Joseph's College, Philadelphia, 1851-1926.* Philadelphia: Saint Joseph's College, 1927.

Warner, Sam Bass, Jr. *The Private City: Philadelphia in Three Periods of Its Growth.* Philadelphia: University of Pennsylvania Press, 1971

PERIODICALS AND WEBPAGES

The Philadelphia *Inquirer* (various)
The Philadelphia *Daily News* (various)
The New York Times (various)

More and More States Embrace Charter Schools - *Education World*, by Colleen Newquist, March 2, 1998
School Vouchers 101: An Overview of This Year's Hottest Campaign Debate - *Education World*, by Diane Weaver Dunne, May 23, 2000

The Society of Jesus in the United States (webpage)
Sisters, Servants of the Immaculate Heart of Mary (webpage)
Charter Schools: An Overview- *U.S. Charter Schools* (webpage)
Answers to Frequently Asked Questions About Charter Schools
Center for Education Reform (webpage)

Index

ABOUT THE AUTHOR

Jerrold K. Footlick is a writer, teacher, and counselor on media and public affairs. He was a Senior Editor of *Newsweek* after serving as Education Editor and Legal Affairs Editor of the magazine. He created and edited *Newsweek On Campus*, a magazine for college students, and edited the International edition of *Newsweek*. He also served as Professor of Urban Studies and Journalist-in-Residence at Queens College, CUNY. He is the author of four books, including *Truth and Consequences: How Colleges and Universities Meet Public Crises*, and the editor of two others. A recipient of the American Bar Association Gavel Award, the National School Bell Award, and the Education Writers Association Award, he was a Pulitzer Prize finalist for civil rights coverage. He was graduated from the College of Wooster and earned a law degree from the Harvard Law School. He and his wife, Ceil Cleveland, who teaches at New York University, live on the North Shore of Long Island and in Durham, North Carolina.